Written by a distinguished historian for Americans of the present, this book takes an exciting new look at Americans of the past.

From the earliest colonists to the men and women of the Civil War, Daniel J. Boorstin shows how people from everywhere created a New World—and how the New World turned people from everywhere into Americans.

Markol

THE LANDMARK HISTORY OF THE
AMERICAN PEOPLE

THE LANDMARK HISTORY

illustrated with prints and photographs

OF THE

AMERICAN PEOPLE

FROM PLYMOUTH TO APPOMATTOX

DANIEL J. BOORSTIN

RANDOM HOUSE · NEW YORK

Author's Acknowledgments

My wife, Ruth F. Boorstin, has given this book the full benefit of her expertise, and her editorial skill and judgment. The book would not have been written without her assistance. My sons, Paul, Jonathan, and David, have offered suggestions. Others who have helped include: Professor John Hope Franklin of the University of Chicago, Dr. Louise C. Wade, Miss Barbara Akin, Mrs. Anne Grant, Mr. Peter Marzio, Mr. Stanley K. Schultz, and Mr. William Sweetland. Miss Karen Tobias of Random House has been principally responsible for finding and collecting the illustrations, in which she has shown great ingenuity and discrimination. Miss Janet Finnie of Random House, having proposed the book to me in the first place, has helped shape it from beginning to end. Her patient, imaginative, and unremitting editing are beyond the power of the author to acknowledge. My friendly colleagues and the research resources of the University of Chicago have, as usual, been indispensable.

*This "family album"
is dedicated with love to
Anna, Louis, and Robert*

CONTENTS

Part Three: American Ways of Growing

Part Four: Thinking Like Americans

Part Five: The Rocky Road to Union

A Word to the Reader

American history is a family album. It amuses and astonishes us to see how different our grandparents and great-grandparents looked, how differently they acted. But a family album also reminds us of ourselves, and helps us understand why *we* look and act and think as we do.

American history is the story of a magical transformation. How did people from everywhere become members of the American family? Men and women from a tired Old World, where people thought they knew what to expect, became the wide-eyed explorers of a New World.

American history is the story of these millions in search of what it means to be an American. In the Old World people knew quite definitely whether they were Englishmen, Frenchmen, or Spaniards. But here it took time for them to discover whether they really were Americans, and if so what that meant.

What does it mean to be an American? To answer that question we must shake hands with our earlier selves and try to become acquainted. We must discover what puzzled and interested and troubled earlier Americans. This is not always the same as what has most interested historians. In this book, therefore, you will find less than in other histories about Presidents and Kings and Treaties. And not one word about Tariffs! But you will, I hope, find more about the kinds of things that Americans were especially good at, and even some of the ways in which Americans failed.

What has been especially American about our ways of living and of earning a living? Our ways of making war and making peace? Our ways of thinking and hoping and fearing, of worshiping God and fighting the Devil? Our ways of traveling and politicking, of importing people, of building houses and cities? These are some of the questions I try to answer in this book.

Discovering America, then, is a way of discovering ourselves. This is a book about us.

D. J. B.

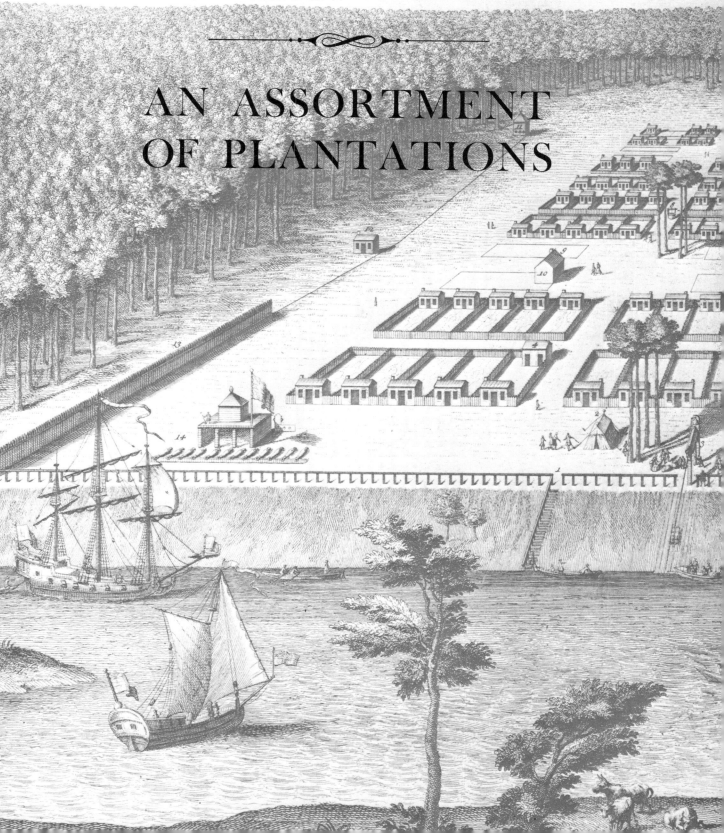

PART ONE

AN ASSORTMENT OF PLANTATIONS

The American colonies were an assortment of dreams and hopes and fears. They offered samples of nearly every kind of feeling. The first settlers, who thought anything was possible here, were not far wrong. Some came with definite plans, others with troubled consciences. Some came as charity cases, owing everything to a few rich men in London. Some came simply for profit. Others came desperately seeking refuge. All would become Americans.

From the beginning America was a place of testing and trying. "Plantations" is what they called the settlements along the Atlantic fringe in the earliest days.

It was a good word. A "plant" first meant a cutting from a growing thing set out to grow in another place. These plantations (we later called them colonies) were European cuttings set out to grow three thousand miles across the Atlantic.

The English were experts at planting people in faraway places. They were never more successful than when they planted in America. For the people here were really *planted*. They did not come only as explorers or as gold diggers. Instead, they took root, found new nourishment in American soil, grew in new ways in the varied American climates, and in a few centuries would outgrow Mother England.

But they were not always successful. Whether a plantation died or lived and how it grew depended on many things. Much depended on the climate and the soil and the animals and the Indians. Much depended on whether the settlers had planned, and what they had planned, and how quickly they could learn what the continent had to teach. And much depended on luck.

CHAPTER 1

The Puritans: Love God and Fight the Devil

America was a land of mystery. Englishmen in the age of King James I knew even less than they thought they knew, because most of their "facts" were wrong. Their misinformation about the New World came in all kinds of packages. Some came in fantastic advertising brochures written by men who wanted to sell land in America.

Men who had put their money and their hopes into new American settlements knew that success depended on attracting people to a strange and remote land. If nobody came, the land would remain a wilderness. But if people did come there would be cities and roads, farms and mines. The wilderness would become valuable real estate. Still more people—more carpenters, shoemakers, tailors, and merchants—would come because they would know they could make a living from the people already here.

The promoters had to offer "facts," but

Virginia, in this seventeenth-century view, was an earthly paradise. Finding fish and game for your table was not hard work, but simply good sport.

they did not know the facts. So they drew imaginary pictures, using ancient legends mixed with their wildest hopes and fondest dreams. The weather in America, they said, was always sunny. The oranges, lemons, apples, pears, peaches, and apricots were "so delicious that whoever tastes them will despise the insipid watery taste of those we have in England." The American venison was so juicy that Englishmen would barely recognize it. The fish were large and easy to catch. In America there were no diseases, and no crowds. Everybody stayed young and everybody could live like a king. Come to this American paradise!

If Englishmen turned to their scientists to check up on all this, they did not get much help. The geography of the New World was quite befuddled. Maps were about as detailed as those we have of Mars—and a good deal less accurate. They had no idea how wide the continent was. When they found a lake or a river near the Atlantic seacoast, they often believed that it would take them to India. When they heard of peculiar animals in America like the raccoon, the opossum, and the bison, which were unknown in Europe, they imagined they must be like unicorns and dragons and other mythical beasts.

When they heard that there were already "red-skinned" men and women in America their religion gave them a ready-made explanation in advance. According to the Bible, all men and women everywhere were descended from Adam and Eve, who once lived in the Garden of Eden. If men in America had red skins, it was simply because of sunburn or dyes. Englishmen took it for granted that the red men in America were one of the ten "lost tribes" of Israel mentioned in the Bible. Because people were so confused about their geography and at first believed that the New World was really a part of India, they had quite naturally called these red people "Indians."

When Englishmen thought about coming to America, one of the questions that interested them most was what sort of

The great "Sea of China and the Indies," this 1651 map showed, was just over the first range of mountains from the Atlantic coast. (The west is at the top.)

people were these American descendants of Adam and Eve who would greet them over here. Would they be friendly and helpful? The rumors were not encouraging. The savages of America, it was said, were not content merely to kill their victims. They delighted in tormenting. They used sharp sea shells to skin their enemies alive, they cut off limbs and joints one by one, and they broiled slices of this human flesh on hot coals. Then they smacked their lips over the sizzling meat before the very eyes of the victims, whom they somehow managed to keep alive. Other Indian cruelties were supposed to be too horrible to tell.

It is surprising that Englishmen dared come to America at all. For in addition to all the real threats of a "hideous and desolate wilderness," they were haunted by these horror stories and nightmares. Against these, all the cheery advertising boasts were not much help. And it is still more surprising that, in spite of all this vivid misinformation, they not only survived but managed to build durable cities.

In the mysterious New World, you would surely be lost unless you had some plans of your own. If you had goals, they could encourage you while you were discovering what America was really like. Your plans had to be definite, but not too definite. You had to be willing to change your plans when you ran into trouble, or when the New World did not offer what you expected. You had to be prepared for disappointment. Yet you had to have unending self-confidence, faith in your mission and in yourself.

In England about the year 1620, some people happened to be equipped with precisely this odd combination of hopes and fears, optimism and pessimism, self-confidence and humility. They were called "Puritans." Their appearance at precisely this time was one of the most remarkable coincidences in history.

Among the Puritans were the Pilgrim Fathers. When they left England in the *Mayflower* on September 16, 1620, they aimed for Virginia. Even before they landed they showed how well they could face the unexpected. At the end of over seven weeks on the ocean they found themselves far north, outside the boundaries where they had permission to settle. Some unruly passengers noticed this, and threatened "that when they came ashore they would use their own liberty, for none had power to command them, the patent they had being for Virginia." But the *Mayflower* leaders, anxious to land, could not tolerate a community without government. Why should their plans be spoiled by a few roughnecks?

So they decided on shipboard, then and there, to create a new government to serve their very special purposes. The leaders, including the steady William Bradford (who would be governor of Plymouth Colony for thirty-one years) and Captain Miles Standish (whom they had hired to head their militia), came together. Like people making up rules for a club that already existed, they wrote out and signed an agreement (or "compact"). This was the famous Mayflower Compact:

In the name of God, Amen. We, whose names are underwritten, the loyal subjects of our dread sovereign Lord, King James . . . having undertaken, for the glory of God,

A European view of the kind of welcome the Indians were apt to give the first settlers.

and advancement of the Christian faith and honor of our king and country, a voyage to plant the first colony in the northern parts of Virginia, do . . . solemnly and mutually in the presence of God, and one of another, covenant and combine ourselves together into a civil body politic; for our better ordering and preservation . . . to enact . . . such just and equal laws, ordinances, acts, constitutions, and offices, from time to time, as shall be thought most meet and convenient for the general good of the colony: unto which we promise all due submission and obedience.

They created an instant government. It worked surprisingly well for the infant colony, and later became the foundation for the great State of Massachusetts.

The Puritans had a grand purpose. In old England they had been called "Puritans" because they wanted to cleanse and purify their church from fancy ceremonies, from rituals which had lost meaning. In New England they wanted to build a Zion in the wilderness. "Zion" was a Hebrew word for "hill," and to the

Puritans it meant the hill where Jerusalem, the first Holy City, was built. Just before the Pilgrims came here, some of them had tried, and failed, to build a purified city in Holland. Now they wanted to try again, far from crowded, decaying old Europe. Perhaps in America they could actually go back to the simpler life of the early days when the first Holy City had been built.

But how would you lay out your city?

What did it all have to do with America—a land that the men of Bible times had never heard of? Some Bible stories are cryptic or complicated, others are bewilderingly simple. Daily life, too, seems complicated, aimless, or confusing. Puritan ministers and teachers tried to find some meaning and make it all less confusing.

To discover this meaning, and the details of God's plan for Zion, the Puri-

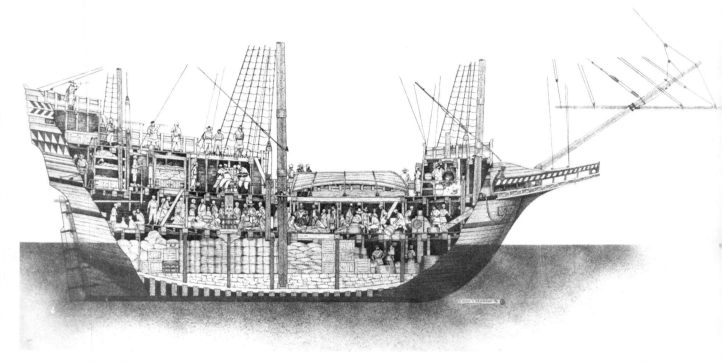

Modern cutaway drawing of the Mayflower *showing the cramped quarters in which the Pilgrims made their seven-week voyage.*

What would you write into your laws? The Puritans, luckily, had a guide. The plan for their community had already been written out, by God himself, in the Bible.

Still, it was no easy matter to find it there. The Bible was a long book, full of stories and poems and prophecies.

tans had a very special way of reading the Bible. For them it was not just a book of quaint tales about people far away and long ago. Instead it was a kind of catalog prepared by God himself, listing all the things that could happen to man. The Puritans believed that everything had, somehow or other, already happened in the stories of the Bible. If you knew how to read the Bible, then, you could find the meaning of what was happening to you today—wherever you were, even in newly discovered America. And from the Bible you could actually predict the future.

The Bible, then, was the key to everything. The Puritans in New England said they themselves were just like the ancient Hebrews, a Chosen People in the Wilderness. The small band of Puritans fighting against scores of Indians were just like little David fighting giant Goliath. And remember that David won!

Everyday events were filled with wonderful meanings. Ministers and teachers helped, but everyone became his own preacher, solving his own Bible puzzles. Some New England leaders kept diaries where they explained these meanings to themselves. Judge Samuel Sewall left one of the best. In his diary for November 6, 1692, he wrote that his little son Joseph threw a brass knob and hit his sister Betty on the forehead, making it bleed and swell. To make matters worse, Joseph did not even repent, but insisted on playing during prayers and actually started eating before grace was finished. Judge Sewall "whipped him pretty smartly" and sent him to bed.

Joseph's grandmother intervened, asking the father to come into the bedroom to forgive his naughty son. "When I first went in (called by his grandmother), he sought to shadow and hide himself from me behind the head of the cradle: which gave me the sorrowful remembrance of Adam's carriage [behavior]."

Judge Sewall at once had found a Bible story to fit his son's misbehavior.

His little son was acting just like Adam in the Garden of Eden. After Adam ate the forbidden apple, he tried to hide from God. Adam knew he had done evil, and that he had something to hide. Puritans called this the "fall" of Adam. Were not all men, and all children too, like Adam? And did this not make it easier to see the dangers of sin, and yet forgive all sinners?

For the Puritans, then, every little fact had a big meaning. And they could be sure, too, that all their little troubles served some large purpose.

There were many advantages to this way of looking at things. You might make mistakes in your own particular explanations and yet believe some purpose was hidden there for you or somebody else to discover. You had just chosen the wrong Bible story to explain your experience. If you ran away from an enemy, you might be escaping from the tyrant Pharaoh. Or then again, maybe you were the sinner Cain, hopelessly wandering after you had killed your brother Abel. Which were you?

Every Bible story was itself a kind of puzzle. You had answered one puzzle with another. But the Puritans were not discouraged. Sometimes, of course, they wondered whether they themselves had actually figured out the meaning of life. But they seldom doubted that there was a meaning to be figured out.

They never doubted that God had assigned them some large purpose—"an errand into the wilderness." If they could not understand the errand, this was only one more proof of how great was God. He alone knew all the answers. The Puritans spent hours listening to

The Burning of Mr. John Rogers

A picture like this enlivened The New England Primer, *from which Puritan school-children learned to read and to love God.*

---

sermons, giving sermons, hearing lectures, and keeping diaries. All these showed both their wonderment over the answers to the daily puzzles and their firm belief that somehow there *was* an answer.

Going to school in New England meant learning God's plan for the Puritans. Children were taught to read from a book called *The New England Primer*. In those days "primer" meant not only a first reader but also a "catechism," or first book of religion. While the young Puritan was learning how to read he was also learning what to believe. Even when he memorized the alphabet it was in little ditties about the Bible. The first item read: "In Adam's fall we sinned all." The last item told about Zaccheus. The pictures did not show "Dick and Jane" chasing their dog Spot across the lawn. Instead they showed the martyr Rogers being burned at the stake while his wife, with nine small children (and holding a baby at her breast), saw her husband give up his life for the true religion.

Harvard College, the first in the English colonies, was founded by the Puritans in 1636. Its main purpose, they said, was "to advance learning and perpetuate it to posterity; dreading to leave an illiterate ministry to the churches, when our present ministers shall lie in the dust." Many Harvard students did not intend to be ministers. But even for them there was no choice about the subjects they studied. Students spent their time on Biblical topics, on difficult Biblical languages (Hebrew, Aramaic, Syriac, and Greek), and on learning how to preach. They discussed God's blueprint for Zion.

Of course it was important to have a plan for building your community. But it was just as important not to expect too much success, and not to expect success too fast. You must expect to succeed, yet you must be more surprised by your successes than by your failures. You would never be disappointed if you were always prepared for the worst.

To explain the Puritans' success in their "hideous and desolate wilderness" we must understand that they were pessimists. Odd though it may sound, they were actually enthusiastic pessimists. For no people has ever believed more strongly in the power of evil. To them the Devil was as real as God. The more powerful the Devil was, the more powerful it proved that God was, because in the long run God always won.

The Indians, according to the Puritans, were armies of the Devil especially equipped to fight against God's Chosen People. No one should be surprised if they were strong or cunning. When Puritans first visited nearby Indian villages they found piles of bones and skulls, reminders of the plague that had hit only a few years before, killing about a third of the Indians in the neighborhood. That plague, the Puritans said, had been specially arranged by God to reduce the Devil's armies and so "make way for the quiet and peaceable settlement of the English in those nations."

Yet the Puritans did not really hate the Indians or believe they were an inferior race. On the contrary, it was a Puritan duty to give "some light to those poor Indians, who have ever sat in hellish darkness." If the Puritans did not convert the Indians to Christianity, the Indians would "go down to hell by swarms without remedy."

John Eliot decided that the best way to convert the Algonquian Indians who lived in the neighborhood was to translate the Bible into the Algonquian language. But the Algonquians had no written language, and Eliot scarcely knew their spoken language at all. By ingeniously using the English alphabet to make the Indian sounds he finally managed to translate the Bible into Algonquian in 1661. That was the first Bible printed in the New World. At Harvard they even built a building called the Indian College to train Indians to be missionaries.

Some Indians took up the Puritans' religion, but still they did not want to change their own way of life. The Indians had the habit of greasing their bodies with fish oil, with the fat of the eagle or the raccoon, or the grease of the bear or the pig. This was useful because the grease protected against heat and cold, and kept off mosquitoes. Also it took the place of clothing. The Puritans noticed only that it was smelly. But they found it easier to persuade Indians to stop following Satan than to stop covering their bodies with grease.

The Puritans believed that the Indian medicine men, who were called "powwows," could actually practice witchcraft. Cautious Puritans like Roger Williams refused to watch the powwows at work because it was dangerous to get so close to the Devil.

When the Indians attacked the Puritan settlements, the Puritans fought back and fought hard. In 1637, because the Pequots (a tribe of Algonquians) were killing settlers and traders, the Puritans made war on them. The war came to an end when Puritans massacred a village of about five hundred Pequot men, women, and children in about half an hour. "Thus did the Lord judge among the heathen," they boasted, "filling the place with dead bodies." They compared this to David's war in the Bible, and proclaimed a day of thanksgiving to God for their victory.

By the time of King Philip's War in 1675, the Indians were more troublesome. The Wampanoag Indians (another Algonquian tribe) had secured firearms from the English and now actually hoped to conquer back the lands taken by the Puritans. This, their bloodiest war with the Indians, was a long fight. Young Puritans had the arrogant notion that one of them could beat ten Indians. They soon learned better. For to win the war against King Philip's tribe, the Puritans had to have the help of some of the Indians themselves. King

Philip (son of Massasoit, an old friend of the Puritans) was finally betrayed by one of his own men.

In many ways the Indians actually helped the Puritans. During their very first bitter winter of 1620–21, the Pilgrims at Plymouth would have died without some reliable advice about how to survive in the American woods.

Squanto was an Indian kidnaped a few years before by an English sea captain, who had sold him into slavery in Spain. He escaped to England, where he learned some English, and then returned to New England in 1619. There he found that his whole village had died of the plague. Now, in March 1621, it was Squanto of all the thousands of Indians in America who happened to turn up in Plymouth! He knew enough English to act as an interpreter. And he showed the Pilgrims how to plant corn (which was not known in England), how to fertilize the soil, where to catch the fish, and how to trap beaver for their fur. No wonder the Pilgrims called him a "special instrument sent of God for their good beyond their expectation."

The Indians helped in still other unexpected ways. When the Puritans needed money to use among themselves and with the Indians, the Indians taught them about "wampum." Wampum was small white or blue-black beads, which had been carved from sea shells. The wampum beads were strung together, and the amount of money they counted for was measured by the length of the string. Using six-foot lengths of wampum, Puritan traders could buy beaver and otter skins from the Indians. During the many years when gold and silver were scarce and they had no paper money, the Puritans traded among themselves by using these odd coins. Even the Devil's own agents could not avoid helping God's Chosen People!

In this mysterious New World, it was easier than in England to give credit for everything to God. Newcomers from Europe did not know what animals or plants or weather to expect here. When New England Puritans found lobsters in the ocean they knew it was God providing for them in their need. When Squanto showed them how to raise corn, he was really God's helping hand. The wild turkey was God's special gift to the Puritans. Was not the turkey unknown in England?

These and all the other provisions of God, the Puritans called "providences." They were God's way of *providing* for his own Chosen People. Over there in England everything had a familiar explanation. In unknown America—still a dark continent—there seemed to be remarkable providences every day.

The Puritans knew it would be a great victory for the Devil if he could discredit God by defeating his Chosen People in the Wilderness. In 1642, when Plymouth Colony suffered a crime wave, Governor Bradford was not surprised or downhearted. "The Devil," he explained, "may carry a greater spite against the churches of Christ and the Gospel here, by how much the more they [the Puritans] endeavor to preserve holiness and purity

Tobacco (at top) and corn (at right) were strange crops that the Europeans learned about from the Indians.

The Indians had much to teach the settlers about hunting.

amongst them." What the Devil most wanted was to "cast a blemish and a stain upon them in the eyes of the world."

In all these ways America gave the Puritans a lively feeling for God—and also sharpened their sense of the Devil. But even the Devil could not drive them to despair. Sooner or later, God would always win. He would see that his own people were not destroyed. The troubles of this world—New England blizzards, Indians' arrows, the plottings of enemies in England, or the crimes of their own sinful New Englanders—never overwhelmed them. They knew too well that *all* men were the children of sinful Adam and had inherited Adam's sin. Man was weak and confused, always giving in to temptations.

The Puritans were not disappointed, then, that they did not build New England quicker. Instead they were surprised and pleased that in a howling wilderness, with the Devil constantly plotting against them, sinful men like themselves actually managed to build anything at all.

So, the saying went, there could never be a disillusioned Puritan—simply because Puritans did not have illusions.

CHAPTER 2
The Quakers Refuse to Fight

In the front and center of a Massachusetts Puritan church was the pulpit. There the learned minister expounded God's plan in the Bible. He gave long and carefully prepared sermons, while the listening congregation took notes. Only those few who had had a very special experience had a voice in running the church. The Puritans called it a "converting" experience, because it converted a sinful soul into one that would be saved in heaven. The converted few were called "Visible Saints." In the early years in Massachusetts, in order to vote you had to be one of these Saints, in addition to having some property. Puritan government was a Dictatorship of the Saints.

In a Quaker meeting house in Pennsylvania, the feeling was entirely different. The whole hall was full of benches. There was no pulpit because there was no minister. In the front a few benches faced the others. Here sat older and more prominent Quakers, called "the weightier members." Their opinions actually carried more weight with their neighbors—but not because they had any high-sounding title or had been anointed as priests. Anyone could sit on the front benches if he felt himself worthy. There was no program, and no regular order of services.

A Quaker Meeting had no chairman, yet it was not noisy or disorderly. Members sat quietly. They waited and waited and waited until someone—anyone— was moved by God's spirit within him. That person would stand up and say whatever God had told him to say, on any subject at all. No one was supposed to prepare anything in advance. And, of course, there was no sermon. If no one felt God's spirit within him, then no one said anything. After sitting awhile, the members would get up and return to their homes.

If there was a practical question, like whether to repair the meeting house roof or where to build a road, the Quakers would not take a vote. Instead, after everybody had had his say, then somehow (without any counting of hands or hearing of voices) members seemed to agree on what was the "sense of the meeting." It is amazing that an organization run this way could run at all. Yet the Quaker Meetings prospered. They gained new members, and for a long time they were the backbone of the new plantation of Pennsylvania.

There was much to be said for this way of running a church. Within the Society of Friends (as the Quakers called their church) it worked surprisingly well. We must remember that each Quaker Meeting was a small number of God-fearing people who knew one another and who shared beliefs. But Pennsylvania was a big place. Within a few years the Quakers' numbers were overwhelmed by others. Many of these disliked or even hated the Quakers. The fringes of settlement were besieged by tribes of Indians and by small armies of French and Spanish. In dealing with this larger world outside, the Quakers did not do so well.

The Quakers who founded Pennsylvania in 1682 were a kind of Puritan. Their leader, William Penn, was the son of a rich British admiral. When he published a pamphlet against the established religion he was imprisoned in the Tower of London, but this simply confirmed him in his Quaker beliefs. He determined to found a colony for refugees in far-off America. A shrewd and persuasive man, he secured a vast grant from King Charles II, which he named Pennsylvania in honor of his father.

Penn's eloquent advertising brochures brought thousands of settlers to Pennsylvania. And much of the prosperity of the colony depended on the sensible constitution that he wrote. He was afraid of neat schemes which could not be changed. "Let men be good," he said, "and the government cannot be bad; if it be ill, they will cure it." He distrusted men who were too bookish, "for much reading is an oppression of

A Quaker meeting house, in America as in England, had no pulpit or altar at the front. An eighteenth-century print by the English illustrator, Thomas Rowlandson.

William Penn is shown here making a treaty with the Indians. The painter, Edward Hicks, was an amateur whose works have a special strength and charm.

the mind, and extinguishes the natural candle; which is the reason of so many senseless scholars in the world."

The Quakers, like other Puritans, wanted to "purify." But they went much further than the Puritans of New England. They were afraid of *any* rules. Even those rules copied from the Bible, they said, would destroy the true religious spirit. Then people would take their religion for granted. God, they said, did not limit his Chosen People only to those who knew the Bible or to those who could read and write. That

was why Quakers had no ministers. They believed in the "universal priesthood of all believers." They believed God had put his spirit into every man, woman, and child. They overflowed with God's spirit. But they were suspicious of anyone who said he knew God's plan.

Just as the Puritans were enthusiastic pessimists, so the Quakers were fanatics about their consciences. Keep looking inward, they said. Let your conscience be your guide. They were afraid of any scheme that was cut and dried, even if some people thought it came from

God himself. God, they said, did not really communicate with man from any printed page. He spoke to each man from within, brightening each man with an Inner Light.

Back in England, the Quakers had been strict pacifists. They opposed war, and refused to fight in any war for any reason, even self-defense. "We are heirs of the gospel of peace," said George Fox, an early Quaker who had gone to jail rather than fight. Fox reminded people that Christ had said, "My kingdom is not of this world." Therefore Christ had told Peter to put away his sword, "for all they that take the sword shall perish with the sword."

It was one thing for Quakers to be pacifists back in England. There they were nothing but a small group of peculiar people. Even if all the Quakers in England refused to fight and went to jail, the country would still be defended. It was quite another matter in Pennsylvania. For there at first the Quakers were a majority. And they ran the Pennsylvania government till the middle of the eighteenth century, long after they ceased to be a majority.

In Pennsylvania, if the Quakers refused to raise an army, the countryside was left defenseless. This is precisely what happened.

The Indians were surely not pacifists. Nor were the French or the Spanish, who were the leading rivals of the British for possession of the New World. The British Empire was continually entangled in wars for America. The English government naturally expected the Quaker colony to bear its share of the war burden. But the Quakers stuck to their pacifism. They would have nothing to do with these colonial wars, even when Spanish privateers sailed up the Delaware River, in sight of Philadelphia.

The most the English government could do was persuade the Quaker legislature in Pennsylvania to use certain dodges, so the Quakers could help defend the colony without violating their pacifism. Once the Quakers pretended they were giving money "to feed the hungry and clothe the naked" Indians, but it was silently agreed the money would be used for defense. In 1745, non-Quakers maneuvered the Pennsylvania legislature into giving £4,000 to supply a military garrison with "bread, beef, pork, flour, wheat, or other grain." It was quietly understood that "other grain" meant a not-very-nourishing grain called gunpowder.

We can understand why American Quakers did not want to join in far-flung wars for empire. What did they care whether the British or the French or the Spanish owned this or that piece of remote wilderness?

It is harder to understand how Pennsylvania Quakers could remain indifferent to the murder of their fellow Pennsylvanians. From the beginning, raiding Indians made life miserable for the backwoodsmen. In 1755 came a terrible climax. During that summer the British General Edward Braddock set out with 1,400 British regulars and 450 colonial troops to take Fort Duquesne from the French. It was strategically located at the river junction where Pittsburgh is now.

Benjamin Franklin, who was shrewd even in military matters, had warned

Braddock against the surprise tactics of the Indians. Braddock, however, was a stiff British general. He believed everybody would follow the genteel rules of European warfare. He thought the Indians would wait till the opposing armies were neatly arrayed in an open field.

But the Indians knew nothing of such rules. Using the surprise tactics which Franklin had predicted, a mixed force of nine hundred French and Indians overwhelmed the British in the Battle of the Wilderness. Braddock was mortally wounded. His chief of staff, the ambitious young Colonel George Washington, after burying Braddock in the forest, took command of the retreating remnant. The French were now in firm control of all western Pennsylvania. They were better situated than ever for inciting the Delaware tribes of Indians to sudden and bloody attacks.

Backwoodsmen now suffered the ravages of total war. Nothing could have been more different from the polite exchanges of musket fire—on prearranged battlefields (in good weather) between professional soldiers—which were called warfare in Europe in those days. American colonists' homes went up in flames, crops were ruined, women and children were scalped or captured. Massacres mounted. Panic gripped western Pennsylvania. Should they stand or run? "Most are willing to stand," reported a citizen in the western town of York

General Braddock, with his British colonial troops in their conspicuous uniforms. At left, hiding behind a rock, is an Indian enemy scout preparing for the surprise attack. Young George Washington was Braddock's chief aide.

in November 1755, "but have no arms or ammunition." Towns farther east were flooded by refugees, while innocent backwoodsmen paid the price for Quaker pacifism.

But the Pennsylvania Quakers still remained pacifists. In their meetings that winter they still refused to give money for defense. They still wanted, as they said, "to walk in white"—to be purer than the pure—even while western Pennsylvania ran red with innocent blood.

In that bloody year of 1755, the Quakers were still very much in control of the government of Pennsylvania. At the beginning of 1756, although Quakers now numbered only one-fourth of the colony's population, they still held 28 of the 36 seats in the legislature. An enraged and exasperated citizenry, led by non-Quakers (and including a number of moderates like Benjamin Franklin), forced the Quakers to resign the government. They never ruled the colony again.

When the American Revolution came, many Quakers stuck to their pacifism. They became gadflies and prophets. They warned against the evils of slavery. Quakers refused to hold slaves themselves, or to buy anything made by slave labor. They opposed alcoholic drinks— and developed the chocolate business in which they prospered.

They were the voice of everybody's conscience. But they were not made for politics.

CHAPTER 3

The Woes of a Charity Colony

The twenty-one men in Great Britain who secured a charter for Georgia in 1732 thought they were very practical. The best known of them was James Oglethorpe, a tough-minded military man who combined a passion for building the British Empire with a passion for reform. He was against strong alcoholic drinks, he wanted to make British prisons more humane, and he opposed slavery. Oglethorpe and his friends had their eyes not so much on the Bible or on their own consciences but rather— so they thought—on the facts and problems of their day.

Their practical worries started right at home in London and reached out to the empire. They were bothered by the "numbers of poor children and other poor that pester the streets of London." They were bothered, too, by the idleness and crime, and especially by the drunkenness. Signs outside some London pubs read: "Drunk for a penny. Dead drunk for two pence." Could not something be done to rid London of its criminal element, its drunken, idle poor?

When they cast their eyes overseas to North America, they saw a vast empty continent where their country was trying to build an empire. On the southern boundaries of the empire, just below the

These were some of the "poor children and other poor that pester the streets of London," as drawn by the bitter English caricaturist William Hogarth. Conditions like these led the London philanthropists to dream of a Georgia haven.

General James Oglethorpe, rugged leader of the Georgia scheme, as sketched in London in his old age.

Carolinas, between the Altamaha and the Savannah Rivers, was a land rumored to be ideally suited for a new paradise. By a happy coincidence, that was precisely where it was most important to have strong armed settlements. For the Spanish had established themselves in Florida farther south, and were always pushing northward.

Of course, the thing to do was to plan a settlement in that area (which they proposed to call "Georgia" after King George II). What could be more obvious? If they planned right they could kill two birds with one stone. They could drain off some of the London poor, while using them in far-off America for a human barricade against the Spaniards who threatened the empire. They could accomplish still another good purpose by setting the poor people to work producing what the empire most needed.

A strong empire, they figured, should grow and make everything for itself. When the British bought anything from another country, British gold drained away and made the other country richer. They measured wealth mainly in gold. All the countries in the world were competing for the world's limited gold supply. Therefore anything that kept British gold at home made Britain stronger.

One problem for a country like Britain —a small island-nation in a cool climate—was that many crops could not be raised at home. Britain had to buy these products from other countries. This weakened the empire by sending British gold abroad. One important product that the British bought from other countries was silk. Every year, as the founders of Georgia pointed out, in order to buy silk the British people were sending out of their country—to the Italians, the French, the Chinese, and others—a fortune in precious metals.

If the British could only produce silk inside their own empire, they would keep all this gold at home. Why not use Georgia? Why not make Georgia into a vast silk plantation?

In London the founders of Georgia embraced this idea with quick enthusiasm. Even before a single silkworm had been taken out to the colony, they announced that silk raising in Georgia would surely give work to at least twenty thousand people there during the four months of the silk season. During the whole year round, they said an additional twenty thousand people in England would be employed making the silk thread into cloth. They predicted that before long all silk worn by Englishmen would be raised in their own empire. The British would soon be exporting silk. They might eventually capture the whole European market.

The longer they dreamed these dreams, the more they discussed them, the more plausible and beautiful the dreams seemed. One special advantage of raising silkworms was that it was not heavy work. It required only a delicate touch and nimble fingers. Did this not make it a perfect employment for the poverty-stricken, undernourished Londoners? Their women and children especially needed work. The Georgia founders happily concluded: "Most of the poor in Great Britain, who are maintained by charity, are capable of this [silk raising], though not of harder labor."

Of what "facts" had the charitable men of London woven this fabric of beautiful illusions? Much of their information had come from earlier advertising brochures. In 1609 some of the adventurers to Virginia (only a few hundred miles north of Georgia) reported finding "silk worms, and plenty of mulberry trees, whereby ladies, gentlewomen and little children (being set in the way to do it) may be all employed with pleasure, making silk comparable to that of Persia, Turkey, or any other." Some of the promoters of Virginia, seeking publicity, had actually presented to King Charles II a coronation robe that they said was woven of Virginia silk.

If the silkworm flourished in Virginia, declared the Georgia promoters in London, surely the silkworm would grow still better in Georgia, because Georgia was farther south. "The air, as it is healthy for men (the latitude about thirty-two)," they advertised, "is also proper for the silk worms." They hired Sir Thomas Lombe, who had become the national expert on silk, to advise them. Lombe had smuggled himself into an Italian silk mill in 1718 in order to steal the secret of silk-making. He had never been to Georgia, but he testified anyway to the sure-fire wonders of silk-raising out there. The promoters of Georgia began to believe their own advertising.

Now the silkworm is a delicate and peculiar animal. It has its own ways, and would not change its diet for anybody—not even to help the suffering poor of London or to protect the great British Empire. It feeds mainly on the leaves of the mulberry tree. But not just any mulberry tree will do. The silkworm feeds only on the *white* mulberry. Unfortunately the Georgia mulberry trees were not of this type. Instead they were *black* mulberry trees, whose leaves do not satisfy the silkworm's choosy appetite. The white mulberry trees would not grow well in Georgia.

This was a little fact which the London promoters had not bothered to notice. It would soon wreck their whole plan for silk-raising. Along with other miscalculations, it would make Georgia's early years a failure.

Plans breed more plans. The ill-informed trustees of Georgia, sitting in their easy chairs in London, went on drawing their plans in ever more minute detail. They required people who received Georgia land to plant mulberry trees in certain quantities. To insure a strong border defense with a well-armed population, each settler had to live near

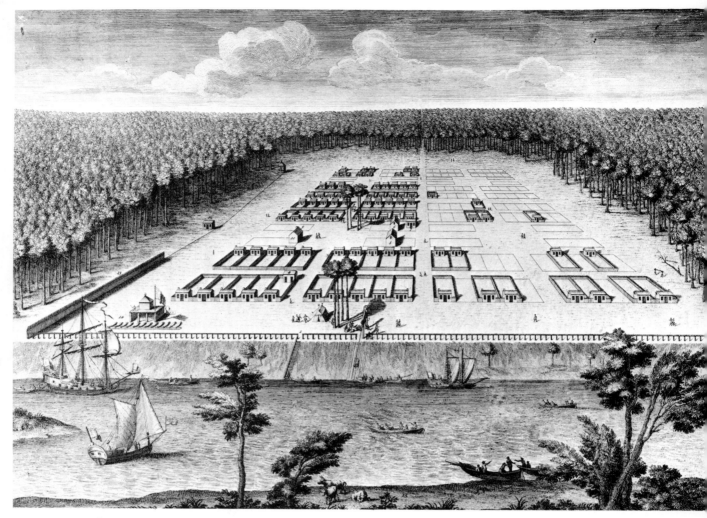

The neat checkerboard scheme which the London planners imagined for the city of Savannah in Georgia (1734).

the others. To keep the settlers sober and industrious the trustees prohibited "Rum, Brandies, Spirits, or Strong Waters." All kegs of liquor in the colony were to be publicly destroyed, and sale of liquor was punished as a crime. No settler was allowed to own or sell the land he worked on. He could use it only according to company rules. No Negro slaves were to be allowed.

This was a charity colony. It was the only colony whose founders did not expect to make money for themselves. To find settlers, they actually advertised for the most worthy charity cases—"such as were most distressed, virtuous, and industrious." Charity cases were in no position to make demands, nor were they allowed to govern themselves or decide what to do with other people's money. Where the people would live, what tools and weapons they would have, what their food rations would be, what clothing they would wear—all these items were settled in England. Georgia became a vast poorhouse. The official storekeeper of the colony (who gave out everything to the settlers) declared that the colonists themselves "had neither lands, rights or possessions; that the trustees gave and that the trustees could freely take away."

A first group of charity settlers arrived in Georgia in 1732. While the high-minded trustees in London made neat rules, the settlers in far-off America had to face the rough facts. They had to live in torrid heat while they tried to farm the pine barrens. They were tempted by slave traders and rum salesmen. They were attacked by Indians and Spaniards. They had to suffer everything. But they could decide nothing.

Since the colony was not operated for profit, when the silk crops failed, the London trustees did not quickly try to find a more profitable crop. Instead they blamed the good-for-nothing settlers, and tried to raise more money to pay for more failures. When the trustees proudly presented to Queen Caroline a gown of "Georgia Silk," it actually had in it only a few, if any, threads from Georgia. The leader of the trustees, Lord Egmont, modestly boasted to the Queen: " 'Tis for persons in high station, who have the means in their hands, to do good."

We cannot be surprised that Georgia did not flourish. An empire-builder's dream turned out to be a nightmare. The settlers rebelled, the trustees gave up. By the time of the American Revolution, Georgia—the spoiled child of charitable London—was the least prosperous and least populous of all the colonies. "The poor inhabitants of Georgia," a settler lamented, "are scattered over the face of the earth; her plantations a wild; her towns a desert; her villages in rubbish, her improvements a by-word, and her liberties a jest; an object of pity to friends, and of insult, contempt and ridicule to enemies."

CHAPTER 4
How British Laws Made Smugglers and Pirates

The settlers who came to New York in mid-May 1623 did not have a grand purpose. They were brought over here by the Dutch West India Company, whose goal was to make money. They called their colony New Netherland, but they did not really want it to be a renewed little Netherland—a new Holland overseas. When the English called *their* settlements New England, they really meant what they said. They expected to build a purified, renewed little England. But not the Dutch. They aimed to set up a trading post and a marketplace.

For Holland was the great merchant of the world. The Dutch were not too particular about what they bought and sold (or sometimes even stole) provided there was a profit in it. And they were not too particular about who came, or what the settlers believed, provided they were willing to trade or to help the Dutch to trade.

The company started dealing in furs, which they gladly bought from Indians or anybody else. Within a year of the

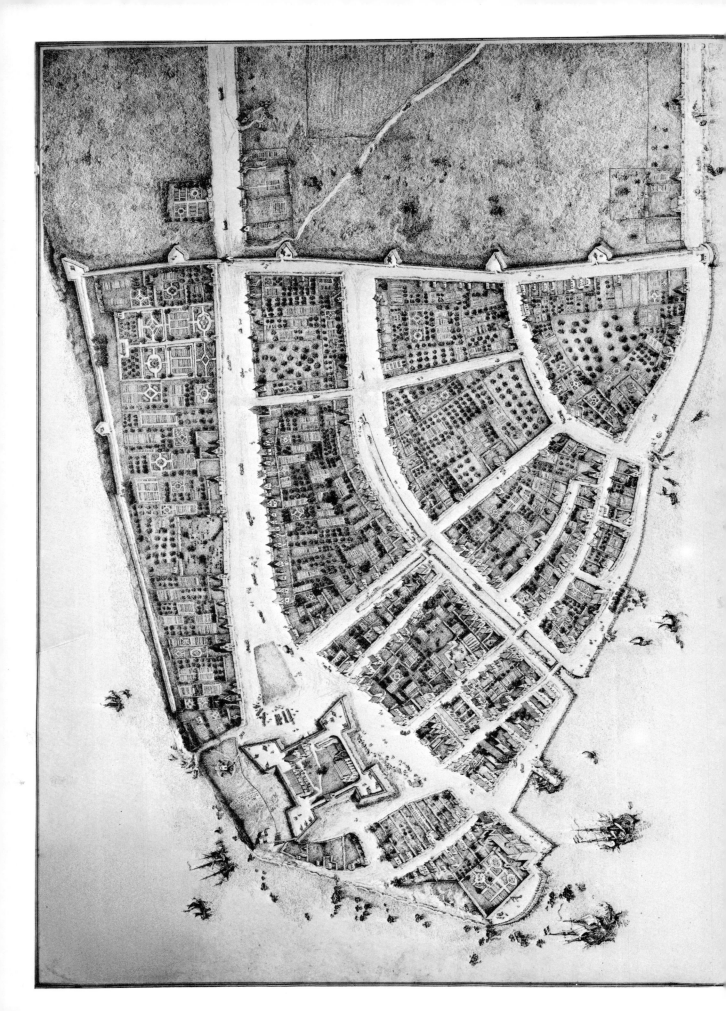

first settlements they sent back to Holland over four thousand beaver skins and seven hundred otter skins. They traded in the tobacco which grew on Manhattan Island. A tobacco plantation stood where we now see the United Nations Building, and Manhattan Island tobacco was as good as the best from Virginia.

The most valuable commodity on Manhattan was, of course, land. Very early the Dutch began "buying" land from the Indians. Fearing they could not establish their right by discovery, the Dutch wanted to be able to say they had actually bought the land from its "owners." The Indians had not settled on Manhattan, but used it only for fishing and for hunting beaver, deer, fox, wild turkey, and the other plentiful game. Not having an idea of landownership anything like that of the Europeans, these Indians probably did not understand what "selling" land to the Dutch meant. The Indians did not know that once the land was sold, the Dutch would have the right to keep them off.

For some trinkets worth 60 Dutch guilders (about $24) several Indian chiefs "sold" Manhattan Island in 1626. Of course, in those days when money was so scarce, $24 was probably worth what several thousand dollars would be worth now. The Dutch were really paying "protection money." They wanted to be allowed to go about their business,

---

New Amsterdam in 1660 (a modern copy of an old map). The fortified wall near the top gave its name to New York's Wall Street. A gate guarded the entrance to the wide thoroughfare known as Broadway.

and one kind of insurance was to try to keep the Indians happy.

The cluster of islands (Long Island, Staten Island, and Manhattan Island) around the mouth of the wide Hudson River provided a safe natural harbor that was less troubled by ice or fog than were other ports in the temperate regions of the world. The broad Hudson River was a superhighway for bringing furs and farm goods from the interior. The city (which the Dutch called New Amsterdam but which became known to history as New York) was conveniently located also for trade to the West Indies and to Africa.

New Yorkers very early began building ships. They built canoes, small sloops (with one mast) and shallops for shallow water, ketches (with two masts), and large yachts. "Yacht" (like "sloop") was originally a Dutch word, meaning a large hunting ship or pirate ship. The beautiful harbor surrounded by virgin timber tempted Peter Minuit in 1630 to finance Belgian shipbuilders in the construction of the *New Netherland*. A ship carrying thirty cannon and displacing some seven hundred tons, it is said to be the largest ship built in America during the next two centuries.

Of the varied enterprises which made New York a great city, none was more profitable than piracy. This began to flourish after the English had conquered New Netherland in 1664 and renamed it New York.

The pirate's trade was a byproduct of certain laws called the Navigation Acts, which the British had passed to make their empire strong. Colonies were supposed to exist not for their own sake, but for the sake of the mother country. The farmers and manufacturers back home in England were the important people. Colonists, therefore, would not be allowed to produce anything to compete. They must not buy from anybody but the English; they must not ship their products to any country but England. Since the English shipbuilding industry had to grow, the colonists must be forced to use English ships.

This was the purpose of the Navigation Acts. Laws beginning in 1650 and coming right down to the era of the American Revolution told the colonists what they could make or raise, what ships they could use, and where they were allowed to sell their products.

Early laws listed only a few items which had to be brought direct from England, but the list gradually became longer and longer. At first goods could be carried in any ships provided these were *owned* by Englishmen, but by 1696, *all* trade between the colonies and England had to be carried in English-*built*

Background: New Amsterdam (New York) twenty years after the arrival of the first Dutch settlers. Foreground: The miscellaneous population of New York included people of many faiths and several races. Here are Quaker tobacco growers from the West Indies.

ships. *All* European goods for the colonies had to come from or through England. The principal colonial products could be exported only to England or to another British colony. Trade with the English or do not trade at all!

It is not surprising that energetic people, who had crossed the ocean and were just beginning to explore the resources of a vast new world, would not let themselves be fenced in. They wanted to ship everywhere and to buy everywhere.

But the Navigation Laws were not regularly enforced. In fact they were largely unenforceable. The British Empire, from the time of the first Navigation Act till the age of the American Revolution, was continually engaged in wars. Sea battles with other European nations—the Dutch, the French, and the Spanish—kept the British navy busy with work more exciting and more urgent than catching a few smugglers. The British navy could not be bothered with the chores of colonial policemen.

Smuggling then became one of the most profitable occupations of the colonial period. It was the foundation of the fortunes of famous American families. Many a nineteenth-century aristocrat looked down his nose at the new immigrants. He said they were enemies of law and order. Yet he perhaps owed his own fortune to smuggling done by his father or his grandfather.

"Privateer" was the name for a legally licensed pirate. The word came into use about 1664, after the first Navigation Acts. It described someone who had a "private" ship which he used for government purposes. The owner of a private vessel in time of war could get a license

from a government official (called a "letter of marque" after the Old French word meaning to seize) allowing him to seize enemy ships. Since he helped the war effort by crippling the enemy, he was allowed by his own king to keep a share of the loot. But when a privateer with letters of marque happened to find a ship with a rich cargo, he was tempted not to take too much trouble to find out its exact nationality.

Once a privateer (or "pirate," to use the less respectable name) had loaded his ship with treasure he would hurry into New York port. In port, he simply showed his letter of marque and explained that he had seized his rich cargo as a patriotic duty to help the war effort. New Yorkers themselves did not want to know whether the goods were really from enemy ships or whether they were simply stolen goods. They were only too glad to have merchandise they could not buy from England, and which they were forbidden to buy elsewhere.

The pirates naturally found New York harbor much to their taste. His Majesty's governor and officers were pleased to have them around. The pirates paid handsome "protection money" to the governor who issued their letters of marque, and who also protected them while they sold their booty.

There were few other places in the world where the market for pirates' booty was so good. Prosperous New Yorkers were ready to pay high prices for all the glittering items—heavily carved and inlaid tables and chairs, filigreed daggers, feathered fans, ornate porcelain, and gold-embroidered cloth—which the pirates had captured from

Busy New York Harbor in 1716.

"enemy" ships trading to the Orient. In this way the unenforceable laws and the unwinnable wars of the British Empire transformed reckless pirates into respectable merchants!

These were not the last pirates or the only kind of pirates who frequented New York City. But no others were more flamboyant. Captains and officers of privateers wore the flashy costume of the new rich. They were hearty and hot-tempered. And they spent money freely—on drink, on women, and on luxuries sold by other pirates. They helped make New York a great, rich, and colorful metropolis.

In colonial New York appeared the most celebrated pirate of modern times: Captain William Kidd. For a while he was one of New York's most respected citizens and a sought-after dinner guest. His success was an example of the wide assortment of new opportunities for enterprise in the New World. His real career was so legendary that it is hard to separate fact from fiction.

When Captain William Kidd arrived in New York City about 1690 at the age of forty-five, he was already a substantial citizen. Son of a Scottish minister, he had risen through the ranks. The fact that he was a privateer did not prevent his being respectable. On the contrary, it proved he was risking his own private ships to punish the King's enemies. The New York colonial legislature voted him £150 for his services!

About the same time that Captain Kidd had established a reputation in New York as a patriotic privateer, King William himself, who was trying to hold together a British Empire that stretched around the world, heard disturbing reports from the Far East. Tales were coming back that out there ships under all flags (some belonging to Englishmen and others to East Indians themselves) were being seized by pirates. One of the headquarters of those pirates, the King learned, was New York. So the King removed the old governor, who had taken bribes to leave the pirates alone, and he sent out a new governor, the Earl of Bellomont.

Bellomont was determined—if possible, at some profit to himself—to exterminate pirates in those far-off Asian waters. He personally organized a company to send ships out to the Indian Ocean to capture the pirates with all their booty. Captain Kidd, whom Bellomont called "a bold and honest man," and who had already proven his ability to chase and capture treasure-laden ships, was Bellomont's choice for the top command. The profits would be spread around—10 percent to the King, the rest shared among Governor Bellomont and the other investors, including, of course, Kidd himself. To divide the booty according to company rules, Kidd had to keep careful records of everything

taken in.

We cannot be surprised that a man of Captain Kidd's active temperament did not relish this work of a bookkeeper. Once in the Indian Ocean he found it both more interesting and more profitable to be a pirate making his own rules (and keeping all the booty) instead of working under company rules to chase pirates for a small commission.

Seizing every ship in sight, Captain Kidd was not careful about whether or not a particular ship was owned by the

A pirate about to be hanged. In those days hangings were a form of public entertainment. (From an English book on piracy, 1724.)

King's enemies. Within two years he became a name to frighten children with. Rumors arriving in England and New York told how the pirate-chaser had become a pirate, how he had plundered innocent villages all over the Indian Ocean. He was said to be ingenious in devising tortures which would persuade the most courageous seaman to reveal the whereabouts of his treasure.

One of Kidd's boldest enterprises, oddly enough, was his final return to New York. There he made a last desperate effort to prove he was not a pirate at all. He actually argued, with elegant technicality, that the ships he captured were all lawful "prizes." Somehow or other, he said, those ships had been under the protection of the enemy French. Bellomont sent Kidd to London, where he was tried for the murder of a sailor and for five instances of piracy. He was hanged on May 23, 1701, still calling himself "the innocentest person of them all." The King confiscated Kidd's property. But rumor has it that the most valuable of all Kidd's treasure still remains to be found—buried in some secret place on an island in New York harbor.

CHAPTER 5

A Scrambling Place— for Refuge and for Profit

There on Manhattan Island began the great American democracy of cash. Nothing is quite so democratic as money (if you have it). It was lucky for us that the city was founded by the Dutch. They were shrewd and ruthless merchants. If you really want to sell something or buy something, you are not apt to bother people with questions about their religion—or about anything else they believe. You are interested only in their money or their goods. The Dutch, therefore, kept their doors open. They let everybody in, and were slow to persecute—not so much because they believed in toleration, but simply because it was good business. New York City became a place of refuge precisely because it was a place of profit.

This also made it a scrambling place. All sorts of people came from all over. The very first settlers whom the Dutch West India Company sent out in 1623 were not Dutchmen at all. They were Walloons—Protestants who came from southern Belgium, where Spanish Catholics were persecuting them—and they spoke French. From New England soon came refugees from the dictatorship of the Puritan Saints. From Virginia came indentured servants, who wanted to exchange the heavy labor of the plantation for the anonymous freedom of the city. And from time to time there came groups of Huguenots, French Protestants who were persecuted in their own country for their religion.

From Brazil came Jews. They were descendants of those who had been expelled from Spain and Portugal by Ferdinand and Isabella in 1492, and they had first sought asylum in the Netherlands before coming to South America. But they needed a new American haven when the Portuguese, who took over Brazil in 1654, threatened them with the tortures of another Inquisition. The stern and narrow-minded Dutch Governor Peter Stuyvesant hesitated to receive them. But the directors of the Dutch West India Company reminded him that the Jews actually held shares in the company. The Jews must be welcomed, provided they looked after their own poor. Then began the privately supported Jewish charities which have flourished ever since in New York.

Religious freedom in New York City was still, by twentieth-century standards, far from complete. With only a few exceptions, Catholics were kept out during most of the colonial period. They were sometimes persecuted on the fancied grounds that they were threatening to take over the government or that they were the natural allies of the French. The Quakers, who came to preach and to convert only twenty years after the colony was founded, were suspected of being anarchists. They were imprisoned and tortured, but they kept coming back. Still, in an age which in Europe was a time of bloody persecution, of religious wars, and of bigotry, New York City was a surprisingly open marketplace of ideas. Anything else was bad business.

Merchants brought with them their Negro slaves, whose number increased until about the time of the Revolution. As early as 1658, a law controlled the treatment of slaves. Some were freed and even owned land. But the city was an excitable place. In 1741, hysteria over the supposed efforts of Spanish Catholics to conquer America was focused on the innocent Negroes. During that summer, fourteen Negroes were burned alive and eighteen were hanged for imaginary crimes. But within another decade that hysteria had passed and Negroes were actually allowed to vote. In 1817 the State of New York voted to abolish slavery.

Big-city politics was turbulent. New York's simmering conglomeration of peoples, languages, and ideas boiled up from time to time. The English, who began fighting to conquer New Netherland as early as 1661, finally occupied the city in 1664. The Dutch managed to reconquer it ten years later, but shortly lost it again to the English. Jacob Leisler, a German merchant adventurer, profiting from the political confusion in England in 1688, seized and held the government of the colony until he was tried and executed for treason in 1691. In 1733, a bold printer, John Peter Zenger, fought for the right to print unpleasant political facts in his newspaper. His trial aroused public enthusiasm and riots. A few years later came the anti-Spanish Catholic hysteria. Then came the Stamp Act riots and the troubled days of the Revolution.

All this helped explain why New York was a place of vitality and of excitement. By 1771 the city had a population of 22,000. People prospered together even while they fought one another.

CHAPTER 6
How a Few Gentlemen Ruled Virginia

In the years before the Declaration of Independence almost nobody, even in America, believed in "democracy." Nobody believed that a man who owned very little property could be trusted with governing himself, much less governing others. Democracy—government by and for all the people—seemed a dangerous word. It meant tyranny and turbulence of the kind we connect with communism or totalitarian government today.

Nearly everybody believed that a man ought to have a good deal of property to vote at all and that he ought to be rich to be qualified for high office. Poor people, it was said, could not be trusted to run a government, because they needed money so badly that they could be too easily bribed. But rich people, the argument went, because they did not need money so badly, were more likely to be honest. It seemed pretty generally agreed that an "honest" government was a government by and for the rich.

Many of the rich and educated who feared the instincts and the power of the common people did believe that a good government somehow had to be a representative (or "republican") government. Of course, they thought, a decent representative government would have to be run by the "better element"—that is, by people with some property.

Most Americans in the era of the American Revolution probably believed in some form of representative government. There were, on the one hand, those who more than anything else

feared the people. Their first worry was to preserve the lives and property and liberties of everybody from the violent whims of the dirty, uneducated masses. On the other hand, there were those who *trusted* the people. They did not yet trust them enough to believe they all ought to be allowed to vote. But they thought the natural instincts of most ordinary people were good. The men they feared most were the men in power.

Much of American history during its early years was a struggle between these two kinds of people: those who most feared the people and those who most feared kings and governors and dictators. The different experiences of the colonial years prepared men to take one side or the other.

Four of the first five Presidents of the United States were Virginia men. These were Washington, Jefferson, Madison, and Monroe. We usually call them the "Virginia Dynasty." They included some of the most powerful leaders who put their faith in the people. How did it happen that in the fifty years just after the Declaration of Independence—when there were thirteen and then more States—so large a proportion of our leaders came from a single State?

One answer lies in some special features of life in colonial Virginia. When these men first learned about government, Virginia was still a colony. James Monroe, the last of the Virginia Dynasty, was seventeen years old at the start of the American Revolution. In colonial

Hogsheads of tobacco being prepared for shipment. This is an illustration for a map made in part by Thomas Jefferson's father, Peter, who was a surveyor. He encouraged his son's interest in map-making.

Virginia, where they had formed their political ideas and habits, these future Presidents had learned to trust the people.

Life in mid-eighteenth century Virginia, when Washington and Jefferson and Madison and Monroe were young men, was extremely cozy—at least for young aristocrats like them. A few families ran nearly everything. They owned the largest tobacco plantations, and tobacco was the foundation of everything else. These same people owned the largest number of slaves. If you wanted to be invited to the most elegant parties, you had to come from one of these families. Sons and daugh-

ters of these families usually married daughters and sons of the same small tobacco aristocracy. It was a good time and place to be alive—at least if your father's name was Burwell, Byrd, Carter, Custis, Harrison, Lee, Ludwell, Page, or Wormley.

We know a good deal about the pleasurable life of the young Virginia blue bloods. They were a well-educated lot, and they kept diaries. Since there was no telephone, they were constantly writing one another letters. When we read the letters which Jefferson wrote in his teens (he was born in 1743, and left us letters written as early as 1760), we can see how different was his life from that of the earlier builders of New Zion in New England, or of the crude backwoodsmen farther west. Almost every name Jefferson mentions was from one of the "best" Virginia families. His first sweetheart, Rebecca Burwell, came from the same Burwell family that had already been running the Governor's Council in Virginia a half-century before.

"Dear Will," young Jefferson wrote to his friend Fleming, "I have thought of the cleverest plan of life that can be imagined. You exchange your land for Edgehill, or mine for Fairfields, you marry Suckey Potter, I marry Rebecca Burwell, and get a pole chair and a pair of keen horses, practice the law in the same courts, and drive about to all the dances in the country together. How do you like it?"

The same Virginians who had played together as children, and partied together when they were young men, ran the government together when they grew up. Whenever the Governor of Virginia tried to fill his Council, he had trouble finding candidates from "suitable" families who were not already overburdened with public offices and government honors. On the list of 91 men who served on the Virginia Governor's Council from 1680 to the American Revolution, there were only 57 different family names. Nearly a third of the councillors were from only nine

Riding to hounds was a favorite sport of the Virginia aristocrats.

different Virginia families.

Many members of these lucky families held more than one office. Sometimes they found themselves actually sitting as judges in cases where they were supposed to hear their own arguments as government lawyers. And besides the colony-wide offices there were many local offices that went to these same families. The young George Washington, for example, was at the same time a church vestryman, a justice of the peace, a commander of the militia, and a delegate to the House of Burgesses. This was an American-style aristocracy, but still an aristocracy.

Since Virginia was a representative government, there had to be elections. These elections of members of the House of Burgesses—the Virginia legislature—were very different from the rough-and-tumble contests we know in modern cities. Nowadays, anybody can run for some office, and nearly everybody can vote. In colonial Virginia, however, everything was organized so that few of the "wrong kind" of people voted and none of them were elected.

Election day was a friendly occasion when George Washington ran for Burgess. To be a voter you had to be a "freeholder"—that is, own land of a certain value. Technically any Virginian qualified to vote could run for the House of Burgesses, but actually no one dared who was not a member of the tobacco aristocracy. There was hardly any campaigning. It was considered rather silly to make a campaign speech since you were appealing entirely to a small number of old friends and neighbors. They had known you since childhood.

It was considered ungentlemanly to solicit votes or to vote for yourself, and there were no organized political parties.

The usual means of persuasion were not complicated arguments or dull statistics about trade and commerce, but large quantities of barbecued beef and pork, served with rum punch and ginger cakes. To persuade people in this way was expensive. Each time he ran for Burgess, Washington spent at least £25, and once his bill came to £50. This was several times what it cost a man in those days to buy the house and land required to qualify him as a voter.

A Virginia law forbade a candidate to offer voters any "money, meat, drink . . . present, gift, reward, or entertainment," but it was seldom enforced. A candidate who entertained his voters lavishly actually proved he was a generous and substantial gentleman. And wasn't that exactly the sort of person you wanted to represent you? Anyway, rich gentlemen were always giving parties. Wouldn't it be ungrateful to accuse them of bribery at election time?

The election itself was a kind of spectator sport. In good weather it was held in the open air on the courthouse lawn. There were no paper ballots. Voting was anything but secret. At the table sat the sheriff, with the candidates, who were expected to be present, and the clerks to count the votes. Each voter came up and announced his choice aloud. Then his vote was recorded on a scoreboard for all to see. As each voter declared his preference, shouts of approval went up from one side and good-natured hoots from the others. The betting odds changed, and new wagers were laid.

In the Governor's Palace, the colonial Governor of Virginia lived in royal style, providing the local aristocracy with a court and social center. Here also lived Patrick Henry and Thomas Jefferson, the first two Governors of the new State of Virginia. Reconstructed on the original foundations at Colonial Williamsburg.

When a candidate received a vote he would rise, bow, and personally thank the voter: "Mr. Buchanan, I shall treasure that vote in my memory. It will be regarded as a feather in my cap forever." When George Washington was running for Burgess in 1758, but had to be away commanding the militia at election time, he sent his friend, the most influential man in the county, to sit at the polls and thank each voter for him.

There was very little danger of voters electing the "wrong kind" of person because the sheriff himself was chosen by the wealthy gentlemen, and the sheriff managed the elections. The sheriff decided who was qualified to vote. He set the date of the election. He decided when voting should begin and (most important) when the voting was closed. If the sheriff's favorite candidate was ahead he might declare the voting closed at two o'clock in the afternoon. But if his candidate was still behind at nightfall he could continue the voting into the next day, while the needed votes were rounded up.

According to Virginia law, a gentleman could vote in every county where he owned enough land. If he owned land in three counties, he could vote three times—once for each of three sets of Burgesses. And he could run for Burgess from any one of the counties where he could vote. A large planter would, of course, choose to run in the most promising constituency. It was normal for Virginians—including George Washington, Patrick Henry, John Marshall, and Benjamin Harrison—to use their large landholdings to help their political careers.

The choice of a Burgess was usually between two equally well-qualified gentlemen from two equally well-to-do families. Virginia, therefore, remained for the whole colonial period in the hands of its "best" people. Slaves or working people could not make trouble at elections. They had no vote. And Virginia had no cities where newly arrived immigrants might vote unpredictably or where vagrant or discontented working people might vote for one of themselves. The largest town in all Virginia during the colonial period was tiny Williamsburg. Although it was the capital, it had a year-round population of less than two thousand people.

Virginia, then, actually was a kind of republic. It did have a representative government elected by "the people." But what a safe and snug republic it was!

Is it any wonder that Virginians like Washington and Jefferson and Madison and Monroe had great faith in what *they*

called representative government? The only kind of representative government they knew was safe and sane—especially for people like themselves who were lords of the tobacco aristocracy. They had a great deal less fear of "the people" and a great deal more confidence that "the people" would select good representatives than did other thoughtful Americans of that age. John Adams of Massachusetts, Alexander Hamilton of New York, and Gouverneur Morris of Pennsylvania—who all lived in or near big cities—knew the fickle, frightening mobs. They put their faith elsewhere.

George Washington wearing his French and Indian War uniform, with the "gorget" of an officer hanging from his neck. By the American artist, Charles Willson Peale, who painted many Revolutionary leaders from life.

Monticello, the house which Thomas Jefferson designed for himself and was continually remodeling. This is the shape he finally gave it, adding the central dome to make it resemble buildings he admired in France and Italy.

Considering how small and cozy was the ruling group, how large was the colony of Virginia (it was the largest colony in square miles, and for most of the eighteenth century had the largest population), and how tightly the aristocracy limited their membership, we must be amazed at how well they ran things. They succeeded partly because they had the same interests. Members of the House of Burgesses, where laws were debated, knew one another intimately. Since newspapers were few and communications were slow, it was hard for Burgesses to be demagogues. In the House of Burgesses the members really debated with one another. They were seldom tempted to speak simply to get votes back home. They discussed what was good for Virginia.

The most valuable power of the House of Burgesses was to give out land. There were vast, unsettled, fertile tracts within the colony which the Burgesses had power to give away—or to sell at a price which amounted to a giveaway. In 1769, for example, George Washington used his influence to extract from the Burgesses a grant of about 200,000 acres (an area about one-third the size of Rhode Island) to his veterans and himself for their service in fighting against the French and the Indians in western Pennsylvania. He even boasted that his men owed all the land they received to his own successful lobbying. Since he had been their commanding officer, he naturally got the largest share.

For the most part, Burgesses were honest men. They believed it was every gentleman's duty to serve in public office. Any man elected Burgess was expected to attend to the public business, and regularly. As early as 1659, a Virginia law fined every Burgess three hundred pounds of tobacco for every day he was absent from the House without a good excuse. Sometimes a man was elected Burgess even when he did not want to run. He was not allowed to refuse the job. In May 1782, the war-weary Jefferson was unhappy because he had been censured for his conduct as Governor during the British invasion. The people of his county elected him a Burgess without his permission. He tried to refuse, but when the Speaker hinted that he might be seized and taken forcibly to Williamsburg, he gave in reluctantly.

The tobacco aristocrats who governed Virginia were, of course, practical men. But to be practical they had to have broad interests. They had to know all sorts of things which a city merchant did not need to know. They had to know about the weather, for the delicate tobacco plant was killed by frost or too much rain. They had to know about the care and breeding of livestock in order to feed their plantation community. Since they were a great distance from big-city doctors or hospitals, they (and their wives, too) had to be amateur doctors in order to give emergency treatment for dysentery or smallpox, or to help deliver a baby. They had to know something about the law (at least as much as an English justice of the peace) in order to decide disputes and punish crimes of the neighborhood. And of course they had to know about politics and the constitution in order to do their job in the House of Burgesses.

If they were going to hear music, they had to know about music, or at least know how to judge musicians. Jefferson imported some Italian grape-raising and wine-making experts who could also entertain his plantation with chamber music. Since their tobacco went from the plantation docks across the ocean to England, Virginia planters also had to know something about world trade and how prices changed with the fortunes of peace and war.

Life in the midst of the remote acres could be lonely and monotonous. When George Washington became bored with seeing the same people day after day, he would send a slave to the nearest crossroad to waylay a passing traveler, to bring him to Mount Vernon for dinner and the night. The proverbial Southern

This "polygraph," one of many ingenious machines devised by Jefferson, made a copy of a letter while the original was being written. In the days before carbon paper and before photocopying, this saved the trouble of making a copy by hand. It was especially useful for Jefferson, who was a prolific letter writer.

hospitality grew in the lonely, isolated plantation whose owner was anxious for fresh company with news from the outside world.

When there were no big-city amusements, and neighbors might be several hours' horseback ride away, men of lively minds turned to books. In 1744, for example, William Byrd's collection of more than 3,600 titles was one of the two or three largest private libraries in North America. Jefferson early in his life began bringing together at Monticello a remarkable library. The whole nation later profited when it became the basis of the Library of Congress. Great libraries like these were, of course, rare. But every plantation had its small collection of books—manuals of farming, religion, law, medicine, and politics for men who had to run their own small world.

Though the men who ran Virginia often turned to books, they were not bookish. They did not read books in order to make learned or witty conversation in somebody's living room after dinner. They were not men of theory. They looked for what was best that could be transplanted from England. Their first goal was to keep Virginia going—to keep the tobacco plantations profitable and at the same time, if possible, to keep workers healthy and happy. Incidentally they learned many things which drew them out to the other colonies, and even to the world. The great Virginians became leading citizens of what was (in Jefferson's own phrase) a world-wide "Republic of Letters."

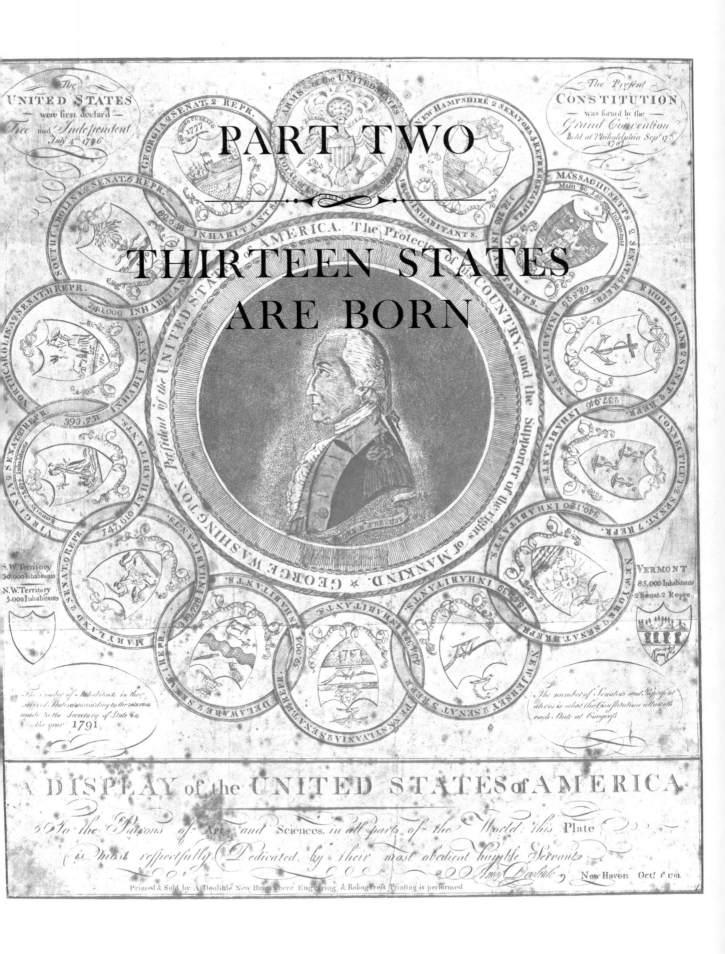

PART TWO

THIRTEEN STATES ARE BORN

Winning the American Revolution, John Adams once said, was like trying to make thirteen clocks strike at once. The colonies were so different that it would have been an astonishing coincidence if they had come to the same idea at the same time. Starting as colonies at different times and with different goals, they moved to independence in thirteen different ways. To bring the people of any one colony—of Massachusetts or Pennsylvania or New York—to agree was difficult enough. To lead thirteen different plantations, to take common action seemed next to impossible. This was the main American problem in the War for Independence.

But this same variety turned out to be a secret weapon in the war. If the Americans were dispersed, if they lacked any single headquarters, this made trouble for the enemy. The colonies were like a monster with many heads. They could survive the loss of several of them. Nothing was more baffling to the British generals. Nothing did more to make it impossible for the British to win the war.

In peacetime, when the new nation was being born, this American peculiarity again became a secret strength.

For here in America it was possible to try many different ways of life within the same country. Not until after the Civil War—a century after the outbreak of the American Revolution—did the States finally decide that they really were a single nation. And that was to be the bloodiest and most painful decision ever made by the American people.

Meanwhile, America was discovering that it was a nation of nations, a people of many peoples. The chance for men and women with two thousand years of Old World civilization behind them to experiment on an unspoiled continent— this was something new under the sun.

To weld these varied communities into a single nation was a chance for a new and unpredictable kind of greatness. The precise character of the nation, like the continent itself, would long remain a mystery. In these next chapters we will see a nation being born. It was born in a puzzling twilight—in the dusk of an old Europe which was the dawn of a new America. Many decades would pass before Americans themselves began to feel sure of the grand outlines of their civilization which was filling a continent.

CHAPTER 7

How the Ocean Tied Some to England

Great Britain—the motherland—was of course an island. Water separated the British from all the world, and water was their only highway to the world. The thirteen American colonies were

also a kind of island. They stretched like a string of beads down the Atlantic seacoast. Every one touched the sea. During the colonial years every important American city was on the Atlantic seacoast, where it could look eastward and oceanward.

What separated every colony from the mother country—and what tied every colony to the mother country—was the ocean. It was the ocean (as Governor Bradford had said) that separated them "from all the civil parts of the world." Westward of the colonies stretched the vast, unfathomed, trackless continent. That was (in a new American phrase) the "back country"—so called because it was away from the ocean. The continent was even more unknown than the ocean and there was no known civilization on the other side.

American independence was, of course, independence from Europe. To become independent meant to turn inland. Future Americans more and more would look and think *westward*. When the inner American continent ceased to be a threat, and became a promise, when the unknown land ceased to be a wall holding them to the sea, and instead became their hope, then (and not until then) did the New World bring forth a new nation. But that was many years coming.

The different feelings of the different American colonies about the mother country and about themselves depended very much on how they used the ocean. Was the ocean mainly a highway connecting them to a modern, civilized homeland? Or was it mainly a gulf separating them from a dying Old World?

The feelings of the different colonies about the ocean depended, of course, on what they hoped to make of themselves. It also depended on what the ocean had to offer them—on how the water came up to their land.

Virginia was a land of riverways. Looked at from the ocean, Virginia had no solid seacoast, but was a half-dozen outreaching fingers of land separated by inreaching fingers of water. In these rich lowlands of "tidewater" Virginia (so called because the ocean tides reach there), the land and the sea seemed perfectly married. Deep navigable rivers—the Potomac, the Rappahannock, the York, and the James—divided Virginia into strips stretching southeastward. Each of these strips was nearly an island. Each in turn was veined by smaller rivers, many large enough to carry traffic to the ocean.

These riverways brought the whole world to the door of every great plantation. From the ocean came ships carrying Negro slaves from Africa and the West Indies, carrying muskets, hoes, clothing, furniture, and books from London. Down to the ocean went ships carrying large barrels (called hogsheads) of tobacco from the broad plantations of the Lees, the Carters, and the Byrds.

Every large plantation had its own dock. Goods arrived there direct from London. Virginians felt little need to have their own cities. For London was their shopping center.

In 1688 an English traveler to Virginia wrote:

No country in the world can be more curiously watered. But this convenience, that in future times may make her like the Netherlands, the richest place in all America, at the present I look on [as] the greatest impediment to the advance of the country, as it is the greatest obstacle to trade and commerce. For the great number of rivers, and the thinness of the inhabitants, distract and disperse a trade. So that all ships in general gather each their loading up and down a hundred miles distant; and the best of trade that can be driven is a sort of Scotch Peddling, for they must carry all sorts of truck that trade thither, having one commodity to pass off [for] another. . . . The number of rivers, is one of the chief reasons why they have no towns.

Planters with riverways running direct to London from their door felt very close to Old England. In those days before railroads, it was slow and expensive to carry anything across the land. "Most houses are built near some landing place," the Rev. Hugh Jones wrote from Virginia in 1724. "Anything may be delivered to a gentleman there [in Virginia] from London, Bristol, etc. with less trouble and cost, than to one living five miles in the country in England; for you pay no freight for goods from London, and but little from Bristol; only the party to whom the goods belong, is in gratitude engaged to freight tobacco upon the ship consigned to her owners in England."

Tobacco was a bulky crop, packed in huge barrels weighing hundreds of

A tobacco plantation was a little village. This painting (about 1825) shows the planter's house on the hill at the center, for it was the center of power and government. Below the slave quarters, barns, and stables is the plantation's own wharf.

pounds. These filled the holds of ships going back to England. What could these ships bring from England? Anything and everything needed by the tobacco planters of Virginia. In the empty holds of ships returning from England, bulky objects could be carried at very little cost. Some wealthy Virginians therefore pleased their families by importing from London heavy furniture and grand coaches elegantly carved and covered with gold leaf.

To make his purchases the Virginia planter naturally had to rely on his agent in London, who was usually the same person who helped him sell his tobacco there. The London agent ran a kind of mail-order shopping service. He supplied all sorts of things—a set of law-books, a fancy bonnet for a wife's or daughter's birthday, a case of wine, a dozen pairs of shoes for slaves.

This man in London (called a "factor," from the Latin word *facere,* to make or do) did almost anything the Virginia planter required. He arranged the English education of the planter's son or daughter, he reported this season's London styles, he sent the latest market news, he advised which recent books were worth reading, and he recounted court scandal or the latest trends in English politics. Sometimes he even helped a lonely bachelor-planter who offered to marry "on fifteen days sight" if the fac-

tor would ship with his other supplies a young woman "of an honest family between twenty and twenty-five years of age; of a middle stature and well-proportioned, her face agreeable, her temper mild, her character blameless, her health good, and her constitution strong enough to bear the change of climate."

Virginia planters thought of themselves not so much as Americans, but as English country gentlemen who happened to be living in America. They still relied on England for books, clothing, furniture, carriages—even for religion and political ideas. During most of the colonial period, the normal way to ship something from a Virginia plantation to Boston was first to send it all the way back to London, from where it would be shipped out to Boston on an English vessel. Virginia Englishmen—including leaders of the American Revolution like George Washington and Thomas Jefferson—owed most of their civilization to England. Many, like Washington, had fought for the King and the British Empire against the French and the Indians.

The ocean which tied them to the English homeland helped them keep the habits and ideas of English gentlemen. With few exceptions they were moderate, sensible men. They would make no trouble so long as they could prosper as loyal Englishmen.

CHAPTER 8
How the Ocean Led Others Out to the World

The same ocean highway that tied Virginia tobacco planters to Mother England led men of Massachusetts Bay elsewhere. The rough and rocky coast of New England offered few gateways to the interior. There were sheltered bays and deep harbors—Salem, Boston, Plymouth, and many others. But New England rivers, with few exceptions, ran steeply downhill. Although they were good for turning a millwheel, they were, for the most part, one-way streets tumbling to the ocean. You could not take an ocean vessel very far inland.

New England bays became havens for big ships that traveled the oceans of the world. On the rocky New England soil, covered by snowy winters far colder than those of Old England, there grew no single staple crop. There was little tobacco, no sugar or silk or rice. New Englanders found their wealth in the sea.

"The abundance of sea-fish are almost beyond believing," Francis Higginson, one of the earliest New Englanders, wrote in 1630, "and sure I would scarce have believed it except I had seen it with mine own eyes." There was fish for every taste: mackerel, bass, lobster, herring, turbot, sturgeon, haddock, mullets, eels, crabs, mussels, and oysters. A small quantity the New Englanders themselves ate. Most they dried, salted, and carried to far parts of the world. Some they sold to the Catholics of Europe, who ate much fish on Fridays. The scraps and leavings went to the slave owners of the Caribbean as cheap food for their Negroes.

Before the end of the seventeenth century, fishing was the main industry of Massachusetts Bay. In 1784, the Massachusetts House of Representatives voted "to hang up a representation of a codfish in the room where the House sit, as a memorial of the importance of the codfishery to the welfare of the Commonwealth." The codfish became the totem of the State. It hung over the Speaker's desk until the middle of the twentieth century.

The New England fisheries actually helped bring on the Revolution. Deep-sea fishermen need ships, and New Englanders began building their own fishing ships in large numbers. This especially worried the English. They feared the colonists would build their own merchant marine and eventually do all their own shipping. And this was one of the reasons why the English clamped the Navigation Acts on the colonies, and went on to tighten their senseless and unenforceable restrictions against colonial trading. Faneuil Hall (which still stands in Boston), the meeting place of the Massachusetts rebels, was given to the city by Peter Faneuil, one of the many merchants who had become rich by shipping New England codfish to forbidden distant markets.

Why should bold and adventurous New England sailors keep inside the boundaries marked off by a few English politicians? Even before the new United States was launched as a nation, New England sailors showed their independence by shipping whatever they could find or make—and to wherever they were carried by whim or profit.

New England ships roamed the world. Their sailors were the first Americans to reach China, where they peddled large quantities of ginseng, a rare herb sup- posed to prolong life. They were the first to reach St. Petersburg in Russia. New England vessels traded with the west coast of Africa, and they went to Zanzibar on the east coast, where they found copal (a substance from tropical trees) to make varnish. They brought the elegant sandalwood (for carved cabi- nets or for burning as incense) from Hawaii. They picked up otter skins in British Columbia on the Pacific, which

Codfish, the mainstay of New England fisheries, were brought to shore in small boats, then dried and salted for shipment. The cannon were intended for protection against Indians or against the French or other imperial rivals.

they carried to China in exchange for the tea which they brought back home for great profits.

Nothing was too small or too big for their commerce or their imaginations. Salem became the world headquarters for trade in the tiny peppercorn, the seed we put in our pepper grinders. Pepper and spices were especially important in the days before refrigeration—both as preservatives and as a cover-up for the foul smell of aging meat. To get oil for lamps, whaling expeditions—which might last three years at a time—went out from New Bedford and Nantucket.

In the days before independence, when English laws still hemmed them in, enterprising New Englanders had to be smugglers. For them, American independence would be a great relief. It would make them into honest, law-abiding men. But long before the American Revolution, the minds and hearts and pocketbooks of bold New Englanders were attached to the whole world.

New Yorkers, too, had their own special reasons for making the ocean a highway away from England. Families of many of the Dutch settlers were still in the Netherlands. New Jersey had been settled by Swedes from the remote Scandinavian north. Pennsylvania had already attracted large numbers of Germans—wagon makers and tailors and cabinetmakers—who still spoke the German language. They naturally wanted German books which could not be found in England. All over the colonies were sprinkled immigrants who had come in groups. Austrians from Salzburg were in Georgia to make silk, Italians in Virginia to teach plantation owners how to raise grapes. Huguenots in Massachusetts and New York and South Carolina were fleeing from persecution in their French homeland. All these learned English only slowly. Their mother country was not England.

Even if colonists had not been independent-minded and determined to run their own lives, the vast ocean barrier would have made them so. The ocean was the father of self-government. The English colonial office, which was supposed to control the governments in the American colonies, had to run its affairs by mail.

Each colony had its own representative assembly. But in each colony the natural leader and the greatest single power was the Governor. He came from England and received his orders from London. The English government in turn depended on him for information about the colony. Getting a message from England to a colony was complicated. Ships were slow and far between. If no ship was sailing, no message could go. The Governor of North Carolina, for example, normally received his communications by way of Virginia. In June 1745 the Board of Trade in London wrote Governor Johnson of North Carolina complaining that it had had no letter from him in the past three years. A full year later he replied from North Carolina that their letter had only just reached him.

During the long New England winter when Boston harbor was frozen or impassable, the whole colony received no word from the outside world. A letter which the Governor of Massachusetts Bay wrote in late November was not

New England sea captains, away on long business trips, caroused in the taverns of the Caribbean—much like modern conventioneers.

likely to reach London before the following April or May. By that time the information it carried would be ancient history. Even if the mail actually reached an English port, there were more delays. It might take weeks or months for mail arriving at Bristol or Falmouth to be carried overland to London. Papers addressed to the Board of Trade were sometimes lost in the customs house, or they might lie for a year before anyone troubled to deliver them.

To avoid these delays of official mail, messages were sometimes sent through friends. Then even the most confidential information might be leaked to people who read the messages on the way.

Parliament was frequently passing laws for the colonies. With nothing but out-of-date information, how could Parliament really know what it was doing?

The continual wars for empire added to all the other difficulties. Britain's enemies aimed to sink all British ships. French and Spanish men-of-war saw that many an urgent government message was delivered to the bottom of the ocean. Not until 1755 was a regular monthly packet boat going back and forth between Falmouth, on the southwestern tip of England (about four hundred miles overland from London), and New York.

By then it was too late. In the American colonies there had already grown up thirteen separate centers of government. Self-government had come to stay, simply from force of circumstance—from the force of three thousand miles of ocean. If Americans wanted to be well governed, they had to govern themselves.

CHAPTER 9

The British Take a Collision Course

The British finally won their colonial war against the French and the Indians in 1763. According to the custom of empires, the loser handed over vast lands and the people in them to the winner. The British Empire was now bigger than ever, which made the thirteen American colonies a smaller part of the empire than ever before. To the north of the thirteen colonies the British had now added all of Canada, and to the south all the regions east of the Mississippi River, including Florida. The people living in these vast lands became new members of the British Empire.

Trouble really began when the well-meaning men running the government in London decided in 1763 to set this far-flung empire in order. Their plans were much too orderly to work well on a continent that was nearly all wilderness. To prevent fighting among the colonies, and to avoid war with the Indians, the men in London decided to try to keep the colonists confined where they already were. The British thought that the Appalachian Mountains, which ran roughly parallel to the Atlantic coastline a few hundred miles inland, would be a useful barrier to keep the colonists separated from the Indians on the west. They proclaimed that in the future the colonists should not settle on the western side of those mountains, and that the Indians should not go eastward.

This was a neat enough idea, but hardly designed to please Virginians, who were always looking for new tobacco land and who were hoping also to make money from wilderness real estate. Was not the continent theirs every bit as much as the Indians'?

At the same time George Grenville, who was in charge of the British treasury (his title was "Chancellor of the Exchequer"), was desperately looking for ways to pay the bills left over from a century of wars. Had not the American colonists eventually profited from the British wars against the enemies of the empire? In the backwoods, colonists had seen their homes burned and their families murdered by French and Indians. On the sea, colonial merchants had lost ships and goods to marauding French and Spanish and Dutch privateers. Why should not Americans now at last pay a fair share of the bills for keeping peace and defending the empire?

Grenville therefore persuaded Parliament to pass the Sugar Act in 1764. It raised the old taxes and imposed many new taxes. Its purpose was not so much to control American trade as to extract American money. That was a fatal mistake. It was the first law ever passed by Parliament to get money from the colonies to send back to support the British government.

This was only the first of a series of disastrous experiments. The British government tried one way after another to get money from the colonies. The men in London raised the taxes on sugar and

Bostonians rejoiced at the burning of British tax stamps.

coffee and wines imported into the colonies. Then, in addition to taxing imports into the colonies, in the Stamp Act of March 1765 they tried a new kind of tax. They now put taxes on all sorts of everyday things which the American colonists used, even if they were not imported. To show you had paid the tax, you would buy a stamp, like a postage stamp. A stamp had to be put on nearly every piece of printed matter in daily use—on newspapers, magazines, calendars, receipts, legal papers for buying and selling land, on ships' papers, on insurance policies, and even on playing cards. If your papers did not have stamps on them they would be seized, you would

be tried (without a jury) and be fined or jailed.

It was bad enough for an ignorant Parliament three thousand miles away to control what came into the colonies. But many colonists still thought that might be a reasonable price to pay for preserving the empire and supporting the British navy. It was quite another matter—and far more serious—when the Parliament in London now started meddling inside the colonies. If Parliament taxed newspapers they could tax books, and then what couldn't they tax? If they could tax everything in the colonies, they could control all daily life. Where would it end?

In a new push to organize trade in the enlarged empire, and to improve business in England, Grenville now also decided to control the trade of the colonies more tightly than ever before. The old Navigation Laws controlling imports and exports had not been strictly enforced. Otherwise Americans would not have tolerated them. Under the new, stricter laws, Americans would be tried *outside* the colonies. They could no longer appeal to juries of their friends and neighbors. And still more laws were added to be sure that no colonial trade leaked to any non-British part of the world.

If these new policies continued, Americans thought, they would no longer be American Englishmen, with all the rights of Englishmen. They would simply be slaves of Parliament. Even in England, some people warned against the new policies.

The colonists quickly replied to British tyranny. They organized town meetings to protest. In order to punish British businessmen, colonists decided not to buy British goods. Some of the richest and most respectable Americans formed a secret society, called the Sons of Liberty, to terrorize the British agents who were trying to sell the hated tax stamps. They persuaded many of the British agents to resign. The Americans used all sorts of arguments, including brickbats and tar and feathers.

Hundreds of merchants in New York City, Philadelphia, and Boston agreed not to buy imported goods until the Stamp Act was repealed. Nine of the thirteen colonies sent official representatives from their colonial assemblies to a special Stamp Act Congress in New York City in October 1765, to combat British tyranny.

All this began to empty British pocketbooks. In a single year, 1764–1765, British sales to America fell off by £305,000.

The London merchants began to worry. To save themselves, they demanded that Parliament repeal the Stamp Act. Benjamin Franklin, representing the colonies in London, went to the House of Commons and warned the British that they were on the road to ruin. If they did not change their policies, there would very likely be rebellion. The Americans, he explained, dearly loved their Mother England, but they loved their liberties even more.

The rulers of Britain might still have saved the situation. If they had known the colonists better, they would have realized that Americans would not let their lives be run by others. A shrewder British government might have worked out a cooperative empire. Then there might never have been a War of Inde-

---

The Sons of Liberty published notices like this to announce their meetings. In those days the letter "s" was sometimes written much like the letter "f."

ADVERTISEMENT.

THE Members of the Association of the Sons of Liberty, are requested to meet at the City-Hall, at one o'Clock, To-morrow, (being Friday) on Business of the utmost Importance;—And every other Friend to the Liberties, and Trade of America, are hereby most cordially invited, to meet at the same Time and Place.   *The Committee of the Association.*

Thursday, NEW-YORK, 16th December, 1773.

pendence. But the rulers of Britain were near-sighted and short-sighted. They thought that government by Parliament had to be all-or-nothing. Unlike the Americans, they were not willing to compromise.

The colonists were practical men. They knew it was possible for Parliament to run their foreign relations, and that Americans could still have their own assemblies—in Massachusetts, in Virginia, and in all the other colonies—to run life inside the colonies.

The men in London did not see it that

This engraving of the "Boston Massacre," as imagined by Paul Revere, became effective propaganda against the British. In the background Revere shows the Old State House (still standing), and in the foreground are the victims.

way. They thought that government by Parliament had to be all-powerful or that it would have no power at all. Even when they repealed the Stamp Act they stupidly declared that Parliament still had power to make laws for the Americans "in all cases whatsoever." They did not realize that a new age had arrived. Two million people were now living in the thirteen colonies. Englishmen in America were beginning to be Americans.

The British government continued its collision course. Needing money at home, they increased the import taxes in America. When colonists resisted, they sent British troops to Boston. All this simply increased colonial resistance.

One of the ablest organizers of colonial rebellion was Sam Adams of Boston. He was a strange man who always had trouble managing his own affairs, but could persuade others how to run theirs. He came from a well-known family and went to Harvard College, where he studied Latin and Greek. His father set him up in business, but he soon lost his father's money. He became tax collector for the Town of Boston, but got into trouble when he failed to hand over all the taxes he collected. He was always in debt, and many Bostonians considered him a shady character.

But Adams made himself a master of propaganda and mob tactics. He was clever at making a sensation out of every incident, and blaming it all on the British. British troops in Boston late one March night in 1770 had been taunted by a few restless unemployed workers. In their confusion, the British troops fired and killed five colonists. Sam Adams advertised this as the "Boston Massacre."

Since it was easier to organize big-city crowds, Boston became a center of agitation. On the night of December 16, 1773, a group of townspeople, who had been organized by Sam Adams, put on the disguise of Mohawk Indians, boarded the tea ships in Boston Harbor, and made their protest against the tea tax by throwing overboard 342 chests of tea. This "Boston Tea Party" helped the Americans prove that it was the principle of the thing and not merely the cost of the taxes that worried them. For the British government had just made complicated arrangements with the British East India Company that reduced the actual price of tea for the American colonists. But at the same time the British government had preserved the hated tax.

Still the British rulers of empire refused to retreat or to compromise. Instead they used force. In 1774 they closed the port of Boston. They seized the government of Massachusetts and then filled the legislature with their stooges. They altogether deprived colonists of the right of trial by jury. They gave British troops in America the power to take over taverns, and even to live free of charge in private homes. The worst American fears had come true.

CHAPTER 10

Americans Declare Their Independence ᕲᕽ

When Americans began to realize that it was hopeless to argue good sense into the heads of the British rulers, they also realized that they were in for a long, hard fight. If thirteen disunited colonies were to win independence from the world's greatest empire, they would need all the help they could find. Most of all, they needed help from the second-greatest empire of the day—France. The French army, and especially the French navy, might make all the difference.

But to win the all-out help of France, the Americans would have to convince the French that the Americans had really cut the British tie—that they were no longer trying simply to patch up a family quarrel. Then France, by helping the Americans, would really be weakening the British Empire. For this reason, if for no other, Americans would have to declare their independence loud and clear.

Until the unpleasantness with the mother country, the colonies had gone their separate ways. There had not been any Congress or any central government where all thirteen colonies could meet and talk about their problems. Franklin and others had tried to persuade them to come together, but with very little success. Now within only a few years the bungling politicians in London did more to push the colonies together than colonial statesmen had accomplished in over a century.

Twelve of the colonies sent delegates (fifty-six altogether) to Carpenters Hall in Philadelphia on September 5, 1774. The meeting called itself the First Continental Congress. It was not really the Congress of any government, for there was no *American* government. It could be nothing more than a *continental* Congress—a collection of delegates from colonies that happened to be neighbors on the same continent.

At first each colony believed it had all the powers of a nation. Yet, because each had been part of the great British Empire, many of the usual jobs of a national government—for example, building an army or a navy, or conducting diplomacy—had been left to London. When the First Continental Congress met, then, it had to start from scratch, taking on many of the jobs of a national government.

The dramatic and disastrous events of April 1775 would put an end to the hopes which some Americans still had that they would somehow find their way back into the empire. Massachusetts

---

Two early battles of the Revolution, shown by two Connecticut artists of the time. Top: Amos Doolittle's matter-of-fact engraving of the British troops marching into Concord, while their commanding officer keeps an eye on the Minute Men. Below: John Trumbull's flamboyant European-style painting of the Battle of Bunker Hill. There the Americans, though forced to retreat, taught British troops to fear militiamen.

had been hardest hit by the British acts of force. And, without waiting for others, Massachusetts began to prepare for war by collecting military supplies in the little town of Concord, about twenty miles inland from Boston.

When the British Secretary of State for Colonies heard of this, he decided to act quickly to destroy that first supply base before the Americans were any better organized. Bostonians learned of the British plan and on the night of April 18, 1775, sent Paul Revere and William Dawes on their celebrated ride to Lexington, which was on the road to Concord. They warned Americans to form ranks to stop the King's troops before these could reach and destroy the colony's Concord supply base. Early the next morning when the seven hundred British troops reached Lexington, they found seventy American Minute Men arrayed against them on the town common. The British killed eight and wounded ten Americans before hastening on to Concord. As if by magic, the countryside sprang to arms. From nowhere appeared thousands of American militiamen. They harassed the British troops, who, before returning to their ships in Charlestown harbor, suffered nearly three hundred casualties.

Now talk was at an end. War had begun. There was no turning back.

When delegates from twelve colonies met again in their Second Continental Congress in the Philadelphia State House in May 1775, they were no longer American children pleading for better treatment from their British mother country. Now they were armed colonists demanding their rights. George

Washington of Virginia was chosen commander in chief of the "Continental Army." It could not be called the Army of the United States, for there was yet no United States.

The Continental Congress quickly realized that they would need a navy. Following the old British example, the Congress, with their own letters of marque, began creating privateers. But now they were *American* privateers in hot pursuit of all British ships. What the Americans most needed was the aid of France, who had a great navy, and, if possible, also the aid of Spain. To encourage this aid, the Continental Congress on April 6, 1776, at one stroke abolished a whole century's accumulation of Navigation Laws. They opened all American ports to all nations in the world, except Britain.

Meanwhile, fortunately for the Americans, who still had no definite word of what was happening in Europe, the French were already conspiring with the Spanish to use this opportunity to tear apart the British Empire. The French King, Louis XVI, secretly arranged to supply gunpowder to the American rebels. From the French the American armies received nearly all the gunpowder they used during the first two years of war. But this was only a beginning.

American independence was already becoming a fact. The Americans had set up their own Congress, they had organized their own army, they were beginning to organize a navy. They had already plainly declared commercial independence by abolishing all the British laws of navigation. Then, on July 2,

1776, the Continental Congress adopted a short resolution "that these United Colonies are, and of right ought to be, free and independent States, that they are absolved from all allegiance to the British Crown, and that all political connection between them and the State of Great Britain is and ought to be totally dissolved."

In many ways this was a mere formality. But John Adams, who had a good sense of history, wrote to his wife on the very next day that July 2 would be "the most memorable" day in the whole history of America. "It ought to be commemorated as the day of the deliverance, by solemn acts of devotion to God almighty . . . with pomp and parade, with shows, games, sports, guns, bells, bonfires, and illuminations, from one end of this continent to the other, from this time forward, forever more."

With the resolution on July 2, Americans had *announced* their independence. They gave out the news that a new nation was born, but they had not yet given out the reasons. Strictly speaking, American independence was not yet *declared*. ("Declare" comes from the Latin word meaning to make clear.) It was not yet officially explained and made clear. And, despite what John Adams said, it was not the mere announcement but the "declaration"— the explanation—of independence that Americans would always celebrate. For Americans were proud of the reasons for the birth of their nation, which they thought were worth fighting for. These reasons gave the new nation a purpose which it would not forget.

One of the remarkable things about the United States, which made it different from the older nations of Europe, was that it could actually point to the reasons why it had become a separate nation. These reasons were listed in a Declaration of Independence prepared and approved by the very men who made the nation independent.

Three weeks before the Continental Congress adopted its brief resolution an-

Thomas Jefferson became an international hero for his authorship of the Declaration of Independence, for his broad scientific activities, and for his faith in the powers of the New World. This portrait bust was made by a French sculptor, Houdon, while Jefferson was serving as ambassador in Paris.

nouncing independence, it had named a committee to prepare a longer Declaration of Independence. The brilliant Jefferson, then only thirty-three years of age, was appointed chairman. Also on the committee were John Adams of Massachusetts and Benjamin Franklin of Pennsylvania, but Jefferson did the writing and the others only changed a word here and there. Some said it was lucky Franklin had not been given the job, for he might not have resisted the temptation to put in a joke. And John Adams, who was also a learned lawyer, might have made the Declaration hard for the average man to read.

Jefferson was the perfect choice. Not only was he a learned lawyer, but he wrote so everybody could understand. And he used phrases that people could not help remembering. He also knew how a new nation ought to explain itself to the world.

The first sign of Jefferson's good sense was that he did not make the Declaration too original. Some years later, John Adams complained that Jefferson's Declaration did not have a new idea in it. Jefferson replied that Adams was correct. The object, Jefferson said, was not to be original, but to say what everybody already believed. He wanted to write down the "common sense" of the subject. The common sense that Jefferson was talking about was not what only the Americans believed. He was speaking to the whole world. It was no good trying to persuade the world unless you started from what lots of people everywhere already believed. That is precisely what Jefferson did.

The opening part of the Declaration, usually called the "preamble," was cribbed from the various books and declarations that Englishmen had written a hundred years before. The English people in England had had a revolution of their own back in 1688. They called it their Glorious Revolution. At that time they had removed one ruler (King James II) who seemed to believe that the nation was his own private property, and then replaced him with King William and Queen Mary, chosen by Parliament.

The British, then, could not possibly deny Jefferson's words in his declaration —that governments derive "their just powers from the consent of the governed." Nor "that whenever any form of government shall become destructive of these ends"—life, liberty, and the pursuit of happiness—"it is the right of the people to alter or to abolish it, and to institute new government . . . in such form as to them shall seem most likely to effect their safety and happiness." Their own British government, as they were repeatedly saying after 1688, was made by precisely that formula. You could hardly call an idea radical if it was the basis of the very respectable government of England.

After the "common sense" in the preamble there came a long list—"a long train of abuses and usurpations." Every item showed how the British King, George III, had disobeyed his own laws. The King aimed to reduce the colonists to "absolute despotism," to establish "an absolute tyranny over these states." His many crimes included "cutting off our trade with all parts of the world," "imposing taxes on us without our consent," and "quartering large bodies of armed troops among us." They also included the King's crimes against the very special rights of Englishmen—for example, taking away the right of trial by jury, and violating the legal charters given to the colonies.

The colonists, Jefferson explained, had shown great respect for their King, and great love for their "British brethren." "In every stage of these oppressions we have petitioned for redress in the most humble terms: Our repeated petitions have been answered only by repeated injury." The King had proved himself a tyrant, "unfit to be the ruler of a free people." If the King would not respect duty to hold the empire together and to protect all his subjects. The Americans demanded nothing but their simple rights as Englishmen. The King had denied those traditional rights. The colonists wanted to preserve them. Now it was not the colonists, but the King, who was really revolutionary.

The King had proved himself a criminal. He did not respect his own laws. How could Americans any longer respect him? The law was now on the side of the Americans. If Americans wondered why they were fighting, here was their simple answer.

On July 4, 1776, Jefferson's Declara-

The French were glad to help American colonists dismantle the British Empire. Here we see the French navy (foreground) in 1778 blockading the English ships (background) in New York Harbor.

the colonists' rights as Englishmen, the Americans had no choice. They had to set up their own government.

Till the very end, Jefferson explained, the colonists had tried appealing to the King. Jefferson's declaration simply ignored the British Parliament. It did not mention Parliament even once. For, according to Jefferson, Parliament had no rights over the colonies. It was the King's tion of Independence was approved by the Second Continental Congress, signed by John Hancock, the president of the Congress, and certified by the secretary. Then copies were sent out to all the States. As new members came to represent colonies in Congress, they too signed the declaration, even though they had not been there when Jefferson first presented it. As late as November some representatives were still signing (there were finally fifty-five signatures altogether). In this way, they showed that they believed in the Revolution.

Congress now sent diplomatic representatives abroad to make treaties and promise commercial benefits in return for help in the war. From all over Europe came officers. Some were really inspired by the American cause, some hated the British Empire, others were simply looking for adventure. From France came the aristocratic young Marquis de Lafayette (commissioned a major general in the American army at the age of twenty!). From Germany came "Baron" de Kalb (also to be a major general) and Baron von Steuben (who became Washington's right-hand man). From Poland came Thaddeus Kosciusko (who built the fortifications at West Point and reached the rank of brigadier general).

In France, Jefferson's Declaration was especially well received. Early in 1778, the French government made a full-fledged treaty of alliance with the Americans—in order to "maintain effectually the liberty, sovereignty, and independence" of the new nation. The French

sent thousands of experienced troops. Without the French navy, the final battle could never have been won at Yorktown. In all these ways, the Declaration of Independence proved a decisive weapon in the war.

That was just what the Americans had hoped. But what they had not expected —and could not even have imagined— was that this eloquent birth certificate of the new United States would fire the imaginations of people all over the world. A few years after the American Revolution was won, when the French people decided to defend their own rights against their king, they found inspiration in Jefferson's words. In the 1820's when Spanish colonists in South America separated from their mother country, they turned to the same source. Jefferson's Declaration of Independence, like other documents that live and shape history, has had the magical power to be filled with new ideas. In the twentieth century, when colonists in Asia and Africa try to explain to the world why they fight for their independence, they still look back to the Declaration of Independence of the thirteen American colonies.

CHAPTER 11
Why the British Lost the War

America produced a new style of warfare. Here the skirmish, not the battle, was important. Communications did not exist, the land was vast. There was no way of directing operations from a cen-

ter. Every man for himself! Colonists had learned to hide behind rocks and tree trunks. "In our first war with the Indians," the Puritan missionary John Eliot noted back in 1677, "God pleased to show us the vanity of our military skill, in managing our arms, after the European mode. Now we are glad to learn the skulking way of war."

Here grew a new and American kind of army. The colonists called it their "militia." The militia was not really an army at all, but only a name for all the citizens who bore arms. As early as 1631, Massachusetts Bay passed a law requiring each town to see that every able-bodied man was armed. Usually each citizen had to buy his own musket. Of course he had plenty of private use for it, hunting game for his table and defending his own house against surprise attack. Regular membership in the militia usually began at about sixteen years of age, and might last till a man was sixty. There was no uniform, and little of the colorful ritual of the European battlefields.

In Europe it was the Age of Limited Warfare. Over there armies fought according to certain definite rules, which made a battle in many ways like a football match. Battles took place on open fields, in good weather. Each side set up its men in neat array. Each side knew what forces the other possessed, and each part of an army was expected to perform only certain maneuvers. To begin a battle before the heralds had sounded their fanfares, to use sneak tactics or unusual weapons, was generally frowned upon.

The only people who fought were the professionals out there on the battlefield. Officers came from the international European aristocracy. They knew the rules and were willing to abide by them. At nightfall, or when the weather was bad, officers from opposing armies would actually entertain one another at dinner parties, concerts, and balls. Then the next day they would take up their places on the battlefield. The privates were human dregs who had been dragged out of jails and bars. The best trained and most reliable soldiers often were mercenaries—like the Swiss or the Hessians—who made a living from hiring themselves out to the highest bidder.

Patriotism had very little to do with those battles. Armies were small. The men were seldom fighting to preserve their country, but more often for some secret purpose known to nobody but the sovereign and his few advisers. By modern standards, the casualties were few. Weapons were crude. The old-fashioned musket had a poor aim, was hard to reload, and would not fire at all in wet weather. Kings could have their battles, and yet interfere very little with the peaceful round of household, farm and fair.

Battles gave nobles a chance to be brave in public while they wore swords, bright costumes, and plumed helmets. Citizens would sometimes stand on the battlements of their town and there at a safe distance watch the colorful clash of arms. War still consisted of a few dramatic battles. It had not yet become a universal misery.

Unfortunately, the American Indian had never heard of these polite traditions of war-by-the-rules. The Indian did not know he was not supposed to use sneak tactics. He especially liked to find a hiding place behind a tree while he surprised his enemy in the dark or in wet weather. For this kind of fighting, the

Indian's simple weapons actually had advantages. Unlike the musket, his bow was silent and accurate, quick and easy to reload. Compared to the European soldier's fifteen-foot pike, his tomahawk was light, easy to maneuver in thick woods, and handy at close range.

The Indian had never heard of the law of war that required him to take prisoners, to treat them kindly according to their rank, and exchange them for prisoners taken by the other side. His custom was to massacre or torture his enemy, sometimes peeling off his skin or bleeding him to death by jabs of pointed sticks.

The Indians conducted a primitive form of total war. And the colonists' only good protection was a primitive form of total defense. When the Indian danger was greatest, whole communities moved into their garrison—a crude fortress-town surrounded by a high stockade. Colonists could not leave their defense to professional soldiers far away on some neat battlefield. Where everybody was a target, every man, woman, and child had to be a soldier. "A grown boy at the age of twelve or thirteen," one back-woodsman noted in the 1760's, "was furnished with a small rifle and shot-pouch. He then became a fort soldier, and had his port-hole assigned him. Hunting squirrels, turkeys, and raccoons, soon made him expert in the use of his gun."

Americans had to defend themselves in their own backyards. They came to believe that every man had a right to carry a gun. In Europe, kings and nobles

---

American soldiers often did not follow the European rules of war. In Germany, when the British (foreground) fought against the French (background) at the Battle of Dettingen in 1743, both sides were in neat array, giving the British a good view of the enemy.

were afraid to let civilians have firearms for an armed people might overthrow the government. When Americans finally wrote their new constitution in 1787, they actually wrote into their bill of rights: "A well regulated militia, being necessary to the security of a free state, the right of the people to keep and bear arms, shall not be infringed." The warfare Americans had learned from the Indians must have seemed very odd to the regular European soldier.

Most remarkable (and most unprofessional by European standards) was the colonial practice of electing officers. This changed the relations between the officers and the men. In the professional armies of the Old World, discipline was not only strict but brutal. Service in the ranks of a European army was a form of punishment for crime. Flogging was the usual means of discipline, food and supplies were meager. But in the American militia, an officer was not likely to be reelected if he treated his men brutally. The relation of officers to men was much more friendly.

Defense of the colonies from south to north depended on these militia groups. They were more like clubs than like what Europeans meant by an army. What a man did in his militia depended on how much he was interested and on what he himself really wanted to do.

Against surprise attacks the militia system could not work unless men came of their own accord, and came on a moment's notice. A visitor to Plymouth in 1627 noticed that men were on the alert day and night. Each man went to

The colonists, who had learned sneak tactics from the Indians (page 19), bewildered and confounded the British by shooting from behind rocks and trees. The British considered such behavior cowardly.

THE AMERICAN RIFLE MEN.

The American militiamen were at first ridiculed, as in this British cartoon, for their lack of discipline and of spit-and-polish.

All this was possible in America only because men here knew what they were fighting for. They were not fighting to preserve a dubious alliance between some king and his cousin, or to gain another spice island for an empire, but to defend their own homes and families.

But still, against a professional army like that of the British Empire, the militia had some grave disadvantages. When American militiamen did not understand the strategy, or when they no longer agreed with the reasons of battle, or when they simply had other personal business, they would give up the fight. The very idea of enlistment—which kept men in the army even when it was personally inconvenient—did not suit militiamen. George Washington's most vexing problems came from these peculiarities of the militia. Since his forces consisted largely of militiamen, he could never be sure how many he could count on.

A large number of the "losses" of Washington's army were due to desertion rather than to death or capture. Within a few weeks before the Battle of Bennington on August 16, 1777 (which helped prepare for the defeat of Burgoyne at Saratoga two months later), over four hundred men deserted. A year later over five thousand militiamen deserted in a few days, so weakening the American forces at Newport that they had to abandon their plan to attack. On March 15, 1781, when the Americans greatly outnumbered the British at Guilford Courthouse in North Carolina, they might have routed the forces of the British General Cornwallis. But the American militia fled to the woods and left

church with his musket in hand, and even during the service he had it beside him. When the Indians attacked in King Philip's War in 1675, an alarm sounded at a town thirty miles outside Boston, and twelve hundred militiamen were there within an hour.

It was the militia that was alerted by Paul Revere and William Dawes in 1775, and that sprang to arms within a few hours in the neighborhood of Lexington and Concord. They had agreed to be ready at a minute's warning. With good reason they called themselves "Minute Men."

victory to the British.

Forces of American militiamen melted away whenever the men decided to go home to help bring in the harvest, or to be present at the birth of a child, or sometimes simply because they were tired of fighting. "Put the . . . militia in the center," the American General Daniel Morgan ordered on one occasion, "with some picked troops in their rear with orders to shoot down the first man that runs." "Militia won't do," he complained. "Their greatest study is to rub through their tour of duty with whole bones."

When General Washington begged the Continental Congress for a regular army organized in the European way, he complained that he had never seen a single instance of militia "being fit for the real business of fighting. I have found them useful as light parties to skirmish in the woods, but incapable of making or sustaining a serious attack."

Militia were a home guard and not an imperial army. That meant they were accustomed to fighting only close to home. But the American Revolution had to be fought wherever the battle required and against a large regular army. A lot of scattered forces, each consisting of a militia "pick-up team" was not good enough. To fight a full-size war you had to be able to send forces far from home. Strategy often demanded that you collect thousands of men for a decisive battle—to destroy the enemy's forces, to seize a dominating hill or an essential port. If Americans were to have a massed army, they had to bring together militia from all over the colonies. But if you sent your own col-ony's militia far away to defend *all* the colonies, you might leave your own colony and your own home naked to the Indians.

Americans in one colony were unwilling to send their militia to help defend a neighboring colony. This was an old story and was an American problem long before the Revolution. The local militia of New York City, organized when it was still New Amsterdam in order to fight the Indians in 1644, would not even go outside the city limits. In midsummer 1691, the Governor of New York wrote asking the Governor of Massachusetts to combine their militias to conquer Canada and so capture the source of the Indian and French marauders that menaced them both. The Governor of Massachusetts begged off with a half-dozen inconsistent excuses, but in return he dared ask the Governor of New York to send some New York militia to help defend Massachusetts from the east. Of course, the Governor of New York also refused.

When Virginia was asked to send its militia north for a common plan of defense, Virginia replied that she had always been her own best defense. And so it went.

In the middle of the eighteenth century, when the British tried to unite colonial troops against the growing threats to all the colonies from the French and the Indians, the British found the task hopeless. Militia of all the colonies together numbered at least ten thousand, but it was impossible to collect them into a single army.

When the American Revolution came, none of this had changed. Each colony still had its own militia—its home guard —but the thirteen colonies as a whole had no army. George Washington's first, and probably his greatest, achievement was somehow to create a Continental Army.

When Washington took command on July 3, 1775, all he had were some thousands of militiamen without uniforms, and without regular military training. It was no easy matter to create discipline. Washington tried to accustom American soldiers to having their officers appointed from above instead of being elected by the soldiers. Since each colony had its own officers, when Washington tried to combine these forces their officers constantly quarreled about who was over whom. In discouragement, Washington reported to the Continental Congress that he could not really say whether he had *"one* army, or *thirteen* armies." Sometimes he had neither and sometimes he had both!

But these crude, disorganized Americans had some special advantages. Of course it was hard to bring the militia together, but that was because they were already spread all over the continent. In vast and trackless America, that itself could be helpful. You did not have to transport all your soldiers. Wherever you were, or wherever the enemy was, a militia was always there.

The militia did not have any uniform. But the fringed hunting shirt of the American backwoodsmen could inspire terror in the regular British soldier. Many Americans used a new and distinctive American rifle which was in every way superior to the old-fashioned British musket. Their ragged costume became

a trademark of the crack shot. General Washington arranged an exhibition of markmanship by men in hunting shirts on Cambridge Common in August 1775, hoping that spies would carry the frightening word of their perfect aim back to the British troops. And he issued an order encouraging "the use of hunting shirts, and long breeches made of the same cloth . . . it is a dress justly supposed to carry no small terror to the enemy, who think every such person a complete marksman."

When the British sent a captured American rifleman back to England as a trophy of the war, his marksmanship actually discouraged recruiting for the war in America. The American militiaman became a legend.

The militiaman's unpredictable behavior made him all the more terrifying. According to the European rules for wars on open battlefields, masses of soldiers were arrayed opposite other masses of soldiers. The European muskets had such poor aim that it was hard for any soldier to pick off a particular opponent. But the sharpshooting Americans disregarded tradition. They aimed especially at the officers. They did not hesitate to use Indian tactics, to sneak up on their enemy, and to hide behind rocks and stumps—all of which was considered cowardly by the rules of the game.

The drab buckskin that Americans wore instead of the colorful uniforms of the British Redcoats made them less conspicuous as targets. Without the spit-and-polish that was the pride of European armies, the rough and ready Americans really did look crude. But they wore no shining brass buttons to reflect light and attract the enemy. Their weapons, which were not burnished for parade or for inspection, were much easier to hide in the woods.

All these peculiarities of the American militiamen helped Americans to haunt and taunt and terrify their better-organized enemy. But even if militia could keep an enemy from winning, could a militia army ever actually *win?* A militia was everywhere. But a militia was also nowhere. Of course, there were tens of thousands of militiamen sprinkled over the colonies. Each was ready to run quickly to defend his home. But where were the massed thousands you needed to repulse a massed British attack?

At the end of the war, George Washington wrote that people in future years would hardly believe that the Americans could have won. "It will not be believed that such a force as Great Britain has employed for eight years in this country could be baffled in their plan of subjugating it by numbers infinitely less—composed of men sometimes half-starved, always in rags, without pay, and experiencing at times every species of distress which human nature is capable of undergoing." Even today it is not easy to understand how the Americans managed to win.

It is easier to explain why the British lost. The British were separated from their headquarters by a vast ocean. Their lines of communication were long. The British government was badly informed. They thought the Americans were much weaker than they really were. And they expected help from uprisings of

Americaner Soldat.

*Accurate Vorstellung eines americanischen Soldaten, von einem Bayreutschen Officir, wel-
dermalen in America, in Englische Dienst befindt, gezeichnet und heraus geschickt wo
Kleidung ist von Zwilch, sie habe lange Gewehr und Bajonet, u, seind sehr dauerhaft u. gesun
Joh. Mart. Will*

The American militiamen soon won a world-wide reputation for marksmanship and hardiness. This is a German drawing of an American soldier wearing fringed buckskin and a hat embroidered with the word "Congress."

thousands of "Loyalists," their name for Americans who refused to join the Revolution. But these uprisings never happened.

The most important explanation was that the British had set themselves an impossible task. Though they had an army that was large for that day, how could it ever be large enough to occupy and subjugate a continent? The British knew so little of America that they thought their capture of New York City would end the war. After the Battle of Long Island in August 1776, General Howe actually asked the Americans to send him a peace commission, and cheerfully expected to receive the American surrender. But he was badly disappointed. For the colonies had no single capital, by conquering which the British could win.

During the first four years of the war, the British managed to capture and hold for some time every one of the four largest cities in the colonies: Boston, New York, Philadelphia, and Charleston. But to snuff out American resistance they would have to control them all at the same time, and then also occupy the stretches of wilderness in between.

It was a long, a very long, war. From the first shot fired at Lexington until the last shot fired at Yorktown, it was nearly eight years. That was almost twice as long as World War I, and a full year longer than World War II. It was a long, slow job to convince the greatest empire with the biggest navy in the world that it should give up.

American success was largely due to perseverance. George Washington was a man of great courage and good judgment. And Americans had the strengths of a New World—with a new kind of army fighting in new ways.

Before they were finished, the Americans did raise their own Continental Army, although there were probably never more than thirty thousand men serving at one time. It is doubtful if the Americans could have won without the aid of France.

Although many Americans opposed the Revolution, and some were lukewarm, it was still a people's war. As many as half of all men of military age were in the army at one time or another. Each had the special power and the special courage which came from fighting for himself, for his family, and for his home.

The very same reasons that made the colonists willing to revolt made them unwilling to unite. The people of Virginia were fighting to be free from a government in far-off London. Why should they submit to a government in far-off New York? The very same feelings that gave Americans strength, that explained why their scattered everywhere-army could not be defeated by a regular army of empire, also explained why it would be hard for them to become a nation. The task of making the nation had only begun.

CHAPTER 12

New States or a New Nation?

Independence had created not one nation but thirteen. At the time of the Declaration of Independence, when John Adams spoke of "my country" he meant Massachusetts Bay, and Thomas Jefferson meant Virginia. The resolution which announced independence on July 2, 1776, had proclaimed "That *these*

United Colonies are, and of right ought to be, free and independent *States.*" The first heading at the top of the Declaration of Independence called it "The unanimous Declaration of the thirteen united States of America." They used a small "u" for united because it was still only a hope.

Each State called itself "sovereign," which meant that now it had all the highest powers of government. Each State had all the powers to levy taxes, to raise an army and build a navy, to enter into treaties, and to make war and peace. When Franklin was in Paris as a representative of the Continental Congress, trying to persuade the French to give war aid, he found "ambassadors" from three separate American States.

Americans like Washington and Madison and Hamilton had seen the troubles of waging a successful war with thirteen different governments. They began to wonder whether thirteen tiny quarrelsome States on the edge of a wilderness could ever prosper—even in peace. Under the so-called Articles of Confederation (in operation 1781–89) which the new States had formed to carry on the war, each State could keep out the farm produce and manufactured goods of its neighbors, much as the British Empire had kept out the products of the French. Instead of facing across the ocean one large power—the British government—hemming in their trade, each of the new little States now found itself surrounded right here in America by a lot of other annoying little States.

The thirteen new American governments had found it impossible to live with a strong London government. They

The New England town meeting, where common problems were discussed and voted on by adult men who owned property. In this way Americans grew accustomed to deciding things for themselves.

now found it almost impossible to live without it. Still nobody wanted to risk replacing the old British tyranny with a new American tyranny. What were they to do?

This was a great moment in history. A few men could shape the world for

After the Revolution each of the thirteen "Sovereign" States issued its own money.

Above: Rhode Island's 60-shilling note. Below: Georgia's 10-shilling note. Both are dated 1786.

centuries. Would America become another Europe? Would the New World become only a new battlefield for thirteen new little nations? Had they risked their "lives, their fortunes, and their sacred honor" only to make the continent into a sea of anarchy?

Wise men, then, dared not let this happen. Their children and their grandchildren, they said, would curse them if they threw away this opportunity to explore together and in peace the vast, mysterious, rich New World.

They decided to come together to talk about their problems. No one thought then of founding all at once a powerful continent-nation. Anyone who proposed that would have been called a silly dreamer. What was in their minds was simply how to prevent thirteen weak nation-states from committing suicide. And how to prevent each little nation-state from strangling the others in a misguided effort to save itself.

In the War of Independence, each colony was fighting to preserve its right to run its own show. When the colonies agreed to cooperate on the War of Independence, they had no idea of making a single new government for a single new nation. What they wanted (as the Governor of Rhode Island had explained) was a "Treaty of Confederation." They were an alliance of thirteen little nations that had come together only to fight the war. Many thought the alliance would disappear after the war was won.

The Continental Congress had begun the war and had declared independence. "The United States in Congress Assembled," which after 1781 carried on the war, was not a Congress of one nation. It was simply a meeting of ambassadors, like the Assembly of the United Nations. Each State had one vote. Every one of the thirteen States had to agree on anything important. Such an assembly of ambassadors could not force any State to support it with money and, of course, had no power at all over individual citizens. It was a miracle that this loose arrangement was able to run a war and force the British Empire to give up.

Then came bad years. As long as the war lasted there had been, as usual in wartime, a business boom. Goods were scarce. Anybody with something to sell found lots of buyers. After the Peace in 1783, Americans were still hungry for the things they could not buy during the war. Once again, they began importing from Great Britain. But they bought a good deal more than they could pay for. Each State issued its own paper money. Nobody knew precisely how much a New York dollar was worth, compared to one from Pennsylvania or Rhode Island. The more money there was, the less a dollar bought. For five long years after 1784 there was the worst business depression the colonies had ever suffered. It was one of the longest and deepest depressions in all American history.

In January 1786, Virginia sent an invitation to all the States to meet and discuss their problems. Nine States accepted the invitation, but only twelve men (representing only five States) actually came to the meeting at Annapolis, Maryland, that September. By then farm workers could barely support themselves on their declining wages.

Moneylenders were seizing farms. In Massachusetts a rebellion was brewing. It was led by Daniel Shays, a now-penniless farmer who had been a captain in the Revolution. To keep order the militiamen of Massachusetts were now being asked to fight against their fellow Americans.

With less than half the States represented at Annapolis there was not much they could do. Luckily, one of the twelve men there was the young, bold Alexander Hamilton. Born of an impoverished family in the Virgin Islands, he had attended King's College (later called Columbia University) in New York, until the Revolution came. During the war, Washington, recognizing Hamilton's brilliance, used him as his close adviser and gave him the job of organizing military headquarters.

Although in 1786 Hamilton was only about thirty years of age, he took the lead. He argued that the thirteen States would never prosper until they formed a strong union. He demanded that, then and there, they send out an alarm to all the States quickly to dispatch representatives to another, larger meeting to see what could be done. If Hamilton had never lived another day, his courage and vision on that occasion would entitle him to a place in American history.

Less than a year later, fifty-five delegates from twelve States met in the hot summer of 1787 in Independence Hall in Philadelphia. The thirteenth State, little Rhode Island (a Boston newspaper called her "Rogue Island"), simply ignored the Convention. It was not at all clear what the delegates were supposed to do. Unlike a convention that the people of Massachusetts had held back in 1780, this meeting had not been called to write a brand-new Constitution. But many members, including especially the two men from Massachusetts, must have remembered the Massachusetts experience. The invitation to this later meeting was vague. The object was somehow to remodel the Articles of Confederation and "to take into consideration the situation of the United States."

Among the many questions that bewildered the fifty-five men in the Convention, the very first was: What power did they really have? But the wiser men did not worry over technicalities. Instead they thought about the job they had to do—to make life better and to make business prosper.

Nothing was newer about the New World than that Constitutional Convention in Philadelphia. This was the first time that there had been a meeting quite like this. History gave them very little to go on.

Despite all the confusion, there was probably one fact on which nearly all the delegates agreed. Each of the States they represented was somehow a "Sovereign" State. That is, the people in each State had *all* the powers to run *all* their own affairs. The American Revolution had been fought to prove it. This was not a mere technicality. It was everybody's starting point. And it was what made the job of the Convention so hard.

What they really had on their hands, then, was a kind of problem in international relations. This was precisely what they meant when they said they wanted to make a new plan for their "federal" union.

In those days "federal" meant something different from what it means today. It was still commonly spelled "foederal," because it came from the Latin word *foedus*, which means "treaty." A treaty was, of course, an agreement made by a "Sovereign" State (or nation). And a "federal" union, then, would be a kind of international association held together by fully Sovereign States which had made treaties with one another. Of course, that would be a very different kind of thing, and would have much less power, than something like the government of England or of France. Could such a weak, loose international association of the thirteen new States do the job for America?

No! was the answer of many delegates to the Philadelphia Convention. Some of the most energetic men—like Alexander Hamilton of New York, James Madison of Virginia, and Gouverneur Morris of Pennsylvania—were sure that would not be good enough. To do the job, the government would have to be "national." That was the word they used, and by it they meant something more or less like the government of France or England.

A "national" union would not be merely a collection of different States, each with its own government. It would be something much stronger. It would actually make laws, have its own courts, levy its own taxes, control commerce, and have supreme power over all the people and all the States under it. Obviously, though, to make that possible, each of the "Sovereign" States would have to give up some of its "sovereign" powers.

It would not be easy to persuade people to this. You would have to ask the people in each State to take powers away from their own Massachusetts, or New Jersey, or Maryland, which the people in that State loved and still called their "country," and give those powers to some imaginary new nation that did not even exist. There were good reasons to fear a powerful new government with its headquarters far outside your State. The best reason of all was the recent bitter experience with King George III and with the British Parliament. But there were other very good reasons for these Americans who had just fought nearly eight years to defend their right to govern themselves.

The thirteen States were very different from one another. What was good for seafaring New England might be bad for tobacco-raising Virginia. And the States were very different sizes. There were vast States like Virginia and New York, which owned unmeasured stretches of wilderness reaching out to the west. And there were small states like Maryland and New Jersey and tiny Rhode Island, which were pushed up against the sea by powerful neighbors.

If under the new plan for a government the States were all to be equal, then the small poor States, with very little to lose, would lord it over the large rich States and make them share their wealth. Or, if the States were all to be

This float honored Alexander Hamilton, in a New York parade celebrating the ratification of the Constitution. Hamilton had represented New York at the Constitutional Convention, and his arguments for a strong central government in the Federalist Papers *helped persuade many doubting Americans.*

unequal, and each State had power in the central government proportioned to its own size or wealth, then what would happen to the little ones?

If any large number of delegates had stuck by their guns and demanded that everything go their way, there would never have been a Constitution. Luckily that did not happen. Although the Convention was held in Philadelphia, which was the headquarters of the uncompromising Quakers, what prevailed in 1787 was the practical spirit of compromise.

Before the Convention had any meetings it was plain that, if there was to be a new government at all, everybody would have to be satisfied with half a loaf. George Washington, who was the chairman of the Convention, was accustomed to bringing people together and solving insoluble puzzles. With the glory of the war behind him, he was able to keep order and keep people on the track. The good-humored Benjamin Franklin, already eighty-one years old, was able to keep people optimistic and keep them talking instead of fighting. Most of the men in the Convention were wise enough to distrust their own wisdom.

The delegates in Philadelphia debated for the whole hot summer of 1787. We do not know exactly what they said, for they had decided in advance to keep everything they said a secret. No complete record was kept. We have to depend on the private notes taken by a few members. But we do know what came out of their meetings. It was the same Constitution of the United States of America which (with only a few amendments) we live under today.

They were able to make a Constitu-tion only because they were ruled by the spirit of compromise. Everybody got something he wanted; nobody got everything he wanted. The big States got a House of Representatives where the big States had more delegates, according to their population; the small States got a Senate, where all States were equal. To satisfy those who wanted a union truly "national," the new government had the power to tax, to control commerce, to make war, to raise an army and a navy, and to carry on foreign relations. To satisfy those who wanted a union merely "federal," the Constitution left to each "Sovereign State" the power to make the laws controlling daily life, and all powers not given to the new central government.

This new government, as one member put it, was "partly national, partly federal." In the Constitution you will not find either the word "federal" or the word "national." The members of the Convention knew that each of these words would be a red flag to some members. They purposely took out these words, and left everybody to guess for himself how much the new government was either federal or national. That way each side could think it had won a little more than the other.

If they did not call the new arrangement either "federal" or "national" what would they call it? Their answer was very wise and very simple. Every time they mentioned the new government in the Constitution, they just called it "the United States."

It was a great enough achievement to make a Constitution that would work in those difficult times. But how can

FEDERAL HALL

The Seat of Congress

Peter Lacour delin.

A. Doolittle Sculpt.

Six years after the end of the Revolution, Americans were united enough to inaugurate George Washington as their first President. The ceremony took place on the balcony of Federal Hall in New York City, then the national capital. An engraving by Amos Doolittle.

we explain the greater miracle, that the Constitution was able to live so long and serve so different an America? Today it is the oldest living written Constitution.

Although this success was miraculous, the explanation is not so difficult. Just as the members of the Constitutional Convention served the people of their own day by being willing to compromise, so they served all of us who came later by being willing to leave some things open. They knew they were building for the future, but they did not know what the future would bring. So they decided to let the future decide many things for itself.

They did this partly by keeping the Constitution short and not trying to list everything. And they purposely left many parts of the Constitution unclear. Precisely what powers would the central government have over the commerce of the States? Could the Supreme Court veto the laws passed by Congress if the Supreme Court thought they were against the Constitution? There is no way of answering these—or many other questions—from the brief few words in the brief Constitution. Let the future make its own definitions!

The members of the Convention were also wise enough to include in the Constitution itself instructions for changing the Constitution. Then, if the people in the future found they needed changes, they would not have to junk the whole Constitution and start all over again. They could keep the Constitution as a whole, while following the rules for making the few amendments they needed. This was a master stroke, and was as new as anything else they did.

When the fifty-five men in Philadelphia finished their work and voted to approve the Constitution, they sent it out to the States. Within less than a year, by June 21, 1788, when New Hampshire approved the Constitution, nine States had accepted. That was enough to put the new Constitution in force.

Since the Constitution was such a patchwork of compromises, we cannot be surprised that it was no easy matter to persuade all the States to adopt it. In every State there were some patriotic and intelligent men (like Patrick Henry in Virginia) who feared a strong new government more than anything else. These men therefore argued against adopting the Constitution. Rhode Island, which had not been represented at all in the Convention, at first refused to join the new government, and did not finally come in until nearly a year after the government was actually working.

The first capital under the new Constitution was New York City. There, on April 30, 1789, George Washington, standing on the balcony of Federal Hall, facing Wall Street, and looking down Broad Street, took his oath of office as the first President of the United States. The motley population of the city which watched him was full of uncertainty and promise and growth.

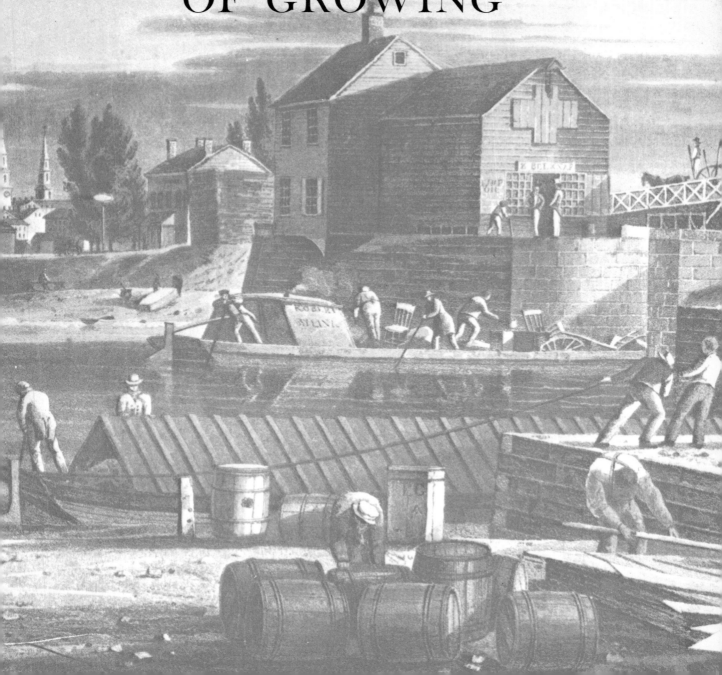

PART THREE

AMERICAN WAYS
OF GROWING

The new nation found its own ways of growing. Other nations had expanded by seizing territory from their rivals, or by sending citizens to far colonies overseas. This is how the great empires had grown. The people back home—in Britain, France, or Spain—added to their own wealth and their opportunities by lording it over distant colonists, making them serve the mother country. But Americans had a vast unsettled empire in their own backyard. Very early they devised a new plan for enlarging their nation by adding neighboring pieces of the continent. Their plan would not make the added people into "colonists," but instead allowed them to become full-fledged, self-governing Americans.

When other nations wanted to increase the population of their homeland, they had to wait for children to be born to the families who had already lived there for centuries. Englishmen were the sons and daughters of Englishmen, Frenchmen the sons and daughters of Frenchmen. But America was the world's leading importer of people. Americans were the sons and daughters of Englishmen, Frenchmen, Irish, Germans, Italians, Asians, and Africans. They were the children of the whole rest of the world. Except possibly for the American Indians, there were no "pure" Americans. The United States attracted its people from everywhere.

In the West before the Civil War, new American cities sprouted by the hundreds. The great European cities—London, Paris, Berlin, Rome, and others—grew gradually by adding to the old residents whose families had lived there for generations. People accustomed to the slow calendar of Europe were astonished to see that in America within only a few years the little raw Western villages had become buzzing metropolises. These instant cities, finding new, quick ways of constructing houses and of building communities, were inspired by extravagant new hopes.

CHAPTER 13

The Add-a-State Plan

Luckily for the nation, there had been two kinds of colonies—"haves" and "have-nots." There were seven "have" colonies: Massachusetts, Connecticut, New York, Virginia, the two Carolinas, and Georgia. Each of these owned vast lands reaching westward.

There was great confusion about some of these Western lands. Sometimes more than one colony thought it owned the very same land. Some had charters from the King giving them a slice of the whole continent all the way to the "Western Ocean," although nobody knew how far that really was. In 1763, the British government tried to take back some of these lands—to confine the colonists eastward of the Appalachian Mountains.

But Americans did not like to be fenced in, and this was one reason for the war.

The remaining six colonies were "have-nots." New Hampshire, Rhode Island, New Jersey, Pennsylvania, Delaware, and Maryland were all hemmed in by other colonies and by the ocean. After Independence they feared their "have" neighbors almost as much as they had once feared the British government. If these six joined a union of such unequal members, they might be bullied and overwhelmed. Weren't they *all* fighting the same war to win all Western lands from the British? And then wasn't it only fair, as the people of tiny Maryland said, that *all* lands "wrested from the common enemy by blood and treasure of the Thirteen States, should be considered as common property"?

Maryland, leading the six "have-not" States, had first refused to join a Confederation with the seven "have" States. Before joining in, she demanded promises that they would all give up their unsettled Western lands. These would go into a treasury belonging to all thirteen States. Virginia began giving up her lands on January 2, 1781. When New York gave up hers two months later,

Jefferson's vision of an Add-a-State Plan (1784). His sketch map proposed 14 future States to be established west of the original 13. (There are now 10 States in this area.)

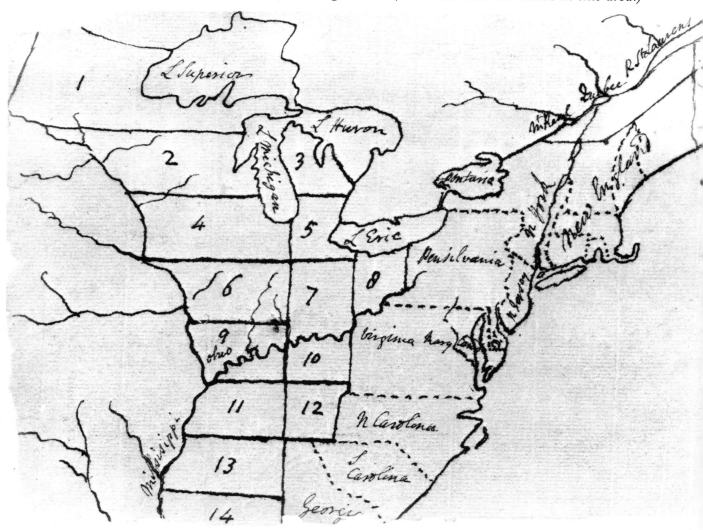

Maryland signed the Articles of Confederation. It was another twenty years before Georgia, the last of the "have" states, fulfilled her promise and put her lands in the common treasury.

Although this argument between the "have" and the "have-not" States was a nuisance at the time, in the long run it was lucky. If all the States had been more equal, each might have kept its own unsettled Western lands all for itself. Then America might have had a very different history. But because the "have" States needed the "have-not" States to help fight the War of Independence, the lands were given to the whole Union.

These Western lands became the treasury of the war. The loose league of States under the Articles of Confederation had no power to tax. Lands took the place of taxes. All the States together owned vast unsettled tracts (called the "public domain") larger than all the settled States put together. By selling the land, the weak new government could get money it could find in no other way. It could even pay the Revolutionary soldiers in land instead of money.

Just as important, the land—whether to be sold or to be governed—would give the new government an important peacetime job. No nation, new or old, had been blessed with such land-treasure in its own backyard. What should be done with it? This unsettled public domain, which belonged to all the States together, was then far larger than France or England or Spain or any other Western European nation.

The Confederation could have made that land into colonies. Just as the British government in London had sent out colonists, while Great Britain remained the mother country and planned the life of the colonies to serve herself, so the original thirteen States could have been a kind of mother country for some new Western colonies. The thirteen Atlantic States then could have used the inland Western colonies to serve them and to make themselves rich and strong.

But the makers of the new nation had seen enough of old-style empires. They preferred to make something quite new. If there was to be any American empire, let it be (in Jefferson's phrase) an "Empire for Liberty." Let it grow in a new way. Why not build this Empire for Liberty by adding one State after another? Each new State would be the equal of each older State. Nowadays this seems an obvious and sensible way for a nation to grow. But in those days it had never been heard of. It was a quite new, American way of growing.

When the seven "have" States began to give up their land, Jefferson began devising a plan. His plan finally became the "Northwest Ordinance." It was adopted by the old Congress of the Articles of Confederation in 1787 at the very time when the makers of a new Constitution were meeting in Philadelphia. This Northwest Ordinance set an American way of growing for centuries to come. It gave instructions for what we can call an Add-a-State Plan.

The plan was simple. Every part of the public domain would eventually become a full-fledged State of the Union, "on an equal footing with the original states in all respects whatsoever." This goal was reached by three simple stages, described in the Northwest Ordinance of 1787. First, when there were still almost no people in a territory it would have a Governor, a secretary, and three judges named by Congress. Then, as soon as there were 5,000 adult free men, there would be a legislature where the people of the territory could make laws for themselves. And finally, when the free population numbered 60,000, the people could apply for admission to the Union as a State.

How many new States should there be? It was anybody's guess. When Jefferson had first started working on his plan back in 1784, he took his map and drew off neat checkerboard squares. He sliced up all Western lands between the boundaries of the Atlantic colonies and the Mississippi River into fourteen new States. But his map was so inaccurate that it did not even have the Great Lakes in the right place! Therefore his plan made very little sense on the real land.

By the time of the Northwest Ordinance in 1787, a little more geography was known. But information was still crude. James Monroe (destined to be President as one of the Virginia Dynasty) took a quick trip out to the Northwest, and he hastily reported back that the land there was "miserably poor." Along the edges of the Great Lakes and around the shores of the Mississippi River and the Illinois River all he saw was vast swamps, separated by "extensive plains which had not had from appearances and will not have, a single bush on them, for ages."

If the land was so poor, then to support a respectable-sized population each new State would have to be much bigger

than Jefferson had planned. The Northwest Ordinance of 1787 therefore prescribed that in the area northwest of the Ohio River there should eventually be "not less than three nor more than five States."

The men who made the Constitution expected the nation to grow, and the States to multiply. They wrote into the Constitution: "New States may be admitted by the Congress into this Union."

In the Constitutional Convention, a few fearful men—Gouverneur Morris of Pennsylvania, Elbridge Gerry of Massachusetts, and some others—distrusted the future. They wanted to write into the Constitution some kind of guarantee that the thirteen old Atlantic States would *always* be more powerful in the government than all the new States put together. Fortunately, the men who looked for and hoped for change, and wanted to encourage new States, prevailed. In the Constitution they also included another promise: "The United States shall guarantee to every State in this Union a republican form of government." In this way they made it plain that the new Union would not be merely a mother country for new colonies.

They also expected people to move around. They were so convinced that this would happen that they actually put into the Constitution some machinery for measuring changes in population. This was the Census. It would keep the government up-to-date. Every ten years there would be a head count, and the number of Representatives of each State in Congress would be changed according to the latest figures. This was something new. It was needed in America if

Centers of population changed as thousands moved westward. This painting by Edward Hicks shows a thriving Quaker farm in western Pennsylvania soon after the Revolution.

the government was to remain really representative.

When the Constitution was adopted, Virginia had more people than any other State; therefore it had more Congressmen in the House of Representatives. But as people moved around and as more came from Europe, things changed. Fifty years later, New York had twice as many people as Virginia. By then Ohio (which did not become a State until 1803) and Pennsylvania each had a half-million more people than Virginia. Before the Civil War more than half the people of the United States were living in States that did not exist when George Washington became President.

In America, change was normal. The power to grow gave the nation the power to live.

After Washington was inaugurated and the new United States began, a procession of new States (in addition to the original thirteen) entered the Union—Vermont (1791), Kentucky (1792), Tennessee (1796), and then Ohio in 1803. All these were carved out of the lands which had belonged to the American colonies when they declared their independence. All were east of the Mississippi River.

Bold Americans like Thomas Jefferson imagined that some day the people of the United States might fill up all the lands between the Atlantic Ocean and the Mississippi.

But anyone who said that the United States would become a continent-nation, with States from ocean to ocean, would have been ridiculed.

CHAPTER 14

An Empire for Liberty

Could the United States remain fenced in forever by those old colonial boundaries? Would the new nation be only a new way of organizing those territories between the Mississippi River and the Atlantic Ocean long ago claimed by the British? Or would the new nation reach out on its own, to enlarge its new-style Empire for Liberty?

The answer came quickly enough—and in a surprising way. No one would have guessed that a New World could be born from the intrigues of the Old. Or that a still larger Empire for Liberty would be born from wars between the Empires of Emperors. But that is how it would happen.

The two leading figures in the story were Napoleon Bonaparte and Thomas Jefferson. Napoleon was a dictator (he called himself "Emperor") who had arisen out of a revolution that failed. Jefferson was a President who had arisen out of a revolution that succeeded. Who could have predicted that Napoleon's thirst for power and glory would give the American President Jef-

ferson his great opportunity to extend the American Empire for Liberty?

It all began because more and more Americans were settling between the Appalachian Mountains and the Mississippi River. They needed transportation. It seemed hopeless to carry produce overland. You had to carry it on your own back or on horseback or by wagon for hundreds of miles up and down the mountains before you could reach the cities on the Atlantic seacoast, where you could sell your crops or buy what you needed. Before the railroad the only cheap and easy transportation was by water.

Western Americans lived far from all the civilized conveniences. But luckily their West was a land of many rivers—the Wisconsin, the Illinois, the Kaskaskia, the Wabash, the Miami, the Ohio, the Cumberland, the Yazoo, and others. These rivers ran into the great Mississippi—"Father of Waters"—down to the Gulf of Mexico and into the ocean. For the Western Americans, these rivers were their highways to the world. But they could reach the outside world only if they had clear passage down and out the Mississippi. If any enemy held the mouth of the Mississippi, he could shut them off.

President Thomas Jefferson understood this very well. His own State of Virginia was a land of many rivers. Jefferson wanted Americans to move out west over the mountains and start new farms. He did not like cities or city life and he believed the Western lands would save America. But who would start a farm if he could not bring in what he needed and send out what he raised? The power to shut off the Mississippi highway was the power to destroy the American West. This worried Jefferson.

Outside the boundaries of the new United States, all the unsettled parts of America were still under the old system of empires. But for Jefferson and other Americans that West seemed a new kind of place—a place to move to, a place to live in, and a place for making a living. For the rulers of Spain and France, the settlers in their far-off American lands seemed nothing but chessmen in a great game of empire-building. The territory itself was for use in a game of diplomacy. They gambled with those American lands and the people on them as if they were not real lands and real people.

When one country won a war it would win another piece of America; if it lost a war it would have to give up a piece. Since the continent was still unexplored, all these bargains were pretty chancy. No king really knew what he was winning or losing, but anyway the game went on. Pieces of America were handed back and forth. When a country "owned"

a part of America, it could do whatever it pleased with the land and it had the power to govern everybody living there.

All America on the western side of the Mississippi River and all the parts around the entrance to the River were being used in this game of empire. Back in 1681, the French explorer La Salle had gone down the Mississippi River and claimed the surrounding territory in the name of King Louis XIV. Calling it after his King, he named it "Louisiana." La Salle claimed all lands drained by the Mississippi, but nobody knew exactly how far that reached.

Then, when the French were defeated by the British in 1763, they handed over to the British all of "Louisiana" east of the Mississippi. Meanwhile, in order to persuade the Spanish to join their war against the British, the French had handed over the rest of Louisiana to Spain. When Jefferson became President in 1801, he began to worry over how to keep open the Western Americans' highway to the world. It looked at first as though he would have to deal with Spain.

But that was not the whole story. Napoleon, who was now in charge of France, had some grand and complicated plans. He had a new scheme to build a French Empire in America. He actually persuaded the Spanish to give him back all of "Louisiana." For reasons of his own, this was done in secret. When word got out that the Mississippi River was no longer controlled by weak and decadent Spain but by the clever, powerful, and ambitious Napoleon, Americans were more worried than ever. And they had good reason. The French soon showed that they knew how to use New Orleans. They made this gateway to the Mississippi into a kind of tollgate. They could, and would, extract whatever they pleased as the price of admission to the Mississippi.

When President Jefferson heard of this he decided that he had to do something at once. He wrote to the American minister in Paris and then sent his friend James Monroe of Virginia as his special ambassador. Jefferson told them to buy from France the land at the mouth of the Mississippi or to find some other way to guarantee that Western Americans could come in and out of their river. If there was no other way, they were to buy New Orleans and all the lands on the east bank of the river (then called West Florida). For this little piece Congress provided two million dollars. But Congress told them they could pay up to ten million dollars if they had to.

Napoleon was a man who made up his mind quickly. He could change his mind just as quickly. Without telling anyone, he had suddenly decided to get rid of his American empire. When the Americans in Paris offered to buy that small piece of land around the entrance to the Mississippi River, they received a reply that astonished them. Napoleon would *not* sell or even rent them that little piece. But he *would* sell them the

---

In the world-wide scramble for empire, Louisiana was a prize. The popular English artist James Gillray showed the British Prime Minister (Pitt) and the French Emperor (Napoleon) greedily carving up the globe.

whole of Louisiana! How much would they offer?

This was the very last answer they expected. They were not prepared for it. Neither President Jefferson nor Congress had imagined it, nor told them what to do if anybody offered them half a continent! But they had to act quickly. Napoleon was a dictator. He did not need anybody's permission for anything. And he expected others to make up their minds just as quickly.

But, unlike Napoleon, the American minister Robert R. Livingston and Jefferson's messenger James Monroe of course had no power to make up their country's mind. What should they do? Should they simply tell Napoleon they could give no answer till they had instructions from the President and Congress back in Washington? That would take weeks —maybe months—and by then the changeable Napoleon might very well say it was all off. Or should they, for the sake of their country, do what they really had no power to do? Should they snatch up this amazing bargain and then pray that the people back home would support them?

This was one of the fateful moments of American history. It was not too remarkable that the dictator Napoleon had made a bold decision. But could Americans with their President and Congress match his boldness? Were the people of a republic doomed to be slow and timid?

Livingston and Monroe took the bold and dangerous way. They decided to take up Napoleon's offer. On their own responsibility they offered fifteen million dollars for all of Louisiana. And he

accepted. As soon as the deal was closed, they began wondering whether what they would have to share was praise or blame. It was some years before either of them dared claim any credit for the decision.

When the news finally reached America it was greeted by shock, delight, astonishment, and dismay. These two Americans, some complained, had been sent to Paris simply to buy a small piece of land to keep the riverways open in the West. Instead of doing that, they had allowed a whimsical dictator to trap them into buying half a billion acres of worthless wilderness! Napoleon was not known for his charities. He was a wily man and, people said, this must be a trick to make innocent Americans serve his evil schemes.

The opponents of President Jefferson (they called themselves "Federalists") said this Louisiana Purchase was typical of the reckless Virginian. They had often accused Jefferson of loving the French, and even of favoring the French Revolution. Now, they said, he was using Americans to help the French sell their undesirable real estate. This was one of the great tests of Jefferson's life.

Jefferson was on the spot. All his life he had been afraid of power and of men in power. He had demanded a bill of rights in the Constitution, to protect citizens from their government. And whenever any question came up, he had said that the central government should not be allowed to do anything that was not listed in the Constitution. If the government could do anything (even though it was not mentioned in the Constitution) simply because it seemed a good idea to the rulers at the time, then there would be no way of ever protecting the people. That was tyranny. That was the way the British tried to rule the colonies. That was precisely why the Revolution was fought, and why there had to be a Constitution in the first place.

But the Constitution said nothing at all about whether or how Congress could buy land from a foreign country. Again and again, in many other cases, Jefferson had argued that Congress had only those powers that the Constitution had given them in so many words. Maybe the power to buy land from foreign countries had been left out of the Constitution *on purpose*—to prevent the United States from playing the dangerous, old-fashioned game of empire. The people of the new United States had tried to escape from the ways of the Old World, where the rulers were in the habit of buying and selling, bartering and gambling faraway lands and unknown peoples.

Now would Jefferson go against everything he had been saying for years? If he had been a weak man he would have been afraid to change his mind. But he decided to show the same courage that had been shown by Livingston and Monroe in Paris. It was harder for him, because he had to stand up and change his mind in public. All his enemies were there to hoot at him. Still, Jefferson decided to go to Congress and ask them to buy Louisiana. He asked them to forget technicalities—"metaphysical subtleties" is what he called them—and instead to think of the future of the nation. He asked them to approve afterwards what they had not been wise enough to approve in advance.

After long and bitter debate, the Congress agreed. In 1803, the Senate approved the treaty with Napoleon. Louisiana became the property of the United States. Within a year, an American Governor was sitting in New Orleans, where he could see that the Mississippi River would stay open. Western Americans would have their highway to the world.

The Louisiana Purchase was a triumph in more ways than we can count. It was one of the first modern proofs that in a battle of wits between a dictator and a government of the people, the popular government does not need to lose. It showed that a people could have a Constitution to protect them against tyrants, and still make speedy decisions. If courageous men did what the nation needed, the people's representatives would approve.

And the Louisiana Purchase provided far more than a mere pathway from Western America to the world. It helped make the new nation itself into a new world. The Louisiana Purchase *doubled* the area of the United States. It made it possible for Americans to keep going west—far across the Mississippi River. It made it possible to carry the Add-a-State Plan westward to the Pacific. It made it possible to build a continent-wide Empire for Liberty. Some men from Eastern States had opposed Jefferson's purchase of Louisiana because they feared that too many new States might be carved out of the West. Then the United States would no longer be an Atlantic-seacoast nation. The original thirteen would no longer run the Union.

Before the nineteenth century ended,

Picturesque New Orleans, after many years under the French and Spanish flags, became even busier as a way station for the new millions in the West. The first State made from the vast Louisiana Purchase was the State of Louisiana, admitted in 1812.

thirteen new States and parts of States would be formed from the Louisiana Purchase. The timid Easterners were wrong in imagining what the United States ought to be. The first thirteen States were nothing but a beginning: a get-on-your-mark line for the spread over North America to the Pacific. There had been other one-ocean nations. Ours was to be a two-ocean nation.

The most wonderful feature of the Louisiana Purchase was the mystery of its boundaries. When we look at a text-book map we sometimes see the Louisiana Purchase clearly marked off. But when Jefferson made the Purchase in 1803, the boundaries were extremely vague. No one, not even Napoleon him-self or Jefferson, knew exactly how far Louisiana reached up north or out west.

Napoleon thought he was very clever to keep the boundaries of Louisiana so vague. Then he could pretend he was selling more than he really owned. Na-poleon could not imagine that those uncertain boundaries would all be gate-ways for new States of the great new American Union. But in this way Napo-leon provided Americans with expand-able boundaries for their Empire for Liberty. The Louisiana Purchase freed Americans from the sharp, confining western boundary of the Mississippi River. The new nation would no longer be imprisoned in the outlines of the antique British Empire.

CHAPTER 15

America's Leading Import: People

With an empty continent to be filled, the United States was more than ever different from the crowded nations of Europe. The Louisiana Purchase itself was seven times the size of Great Britain, four times the size of France or Spain. Yet it had in it fewer people than a single big city of the Old World. During the eighteenth and early nineteenth centuries, European nations doubled their people. But how could they increase their land? The nations were jostling one another. Over there, any little piece of ground was a treasure to be fought over. Nations marked off their boundaries with forts and armies.

It was not surprising, then, that the United States became a nation of immigrants. While Europe became more and more crowded, America offered open air and cheap land. When a man in Europe could not find food for his family or a place for his children in school or as apprentices, he naturally thought of America. In Europe, too, it was an age of turmoil. Between the time of the American Revolution and the American Civil War, there were revolutions and dictatorships in France, Spain, Germany, Greece, Italy, and Belgium. And it was an age of floods and famine. There were lots of reasons why people in Europe might want to get *away from* their Old World. The disasters of Europe made refugees by the millions.

And there were plenty of reasons why someone would want to come *to* America. Of course, there were all the old legends started in the early advertising brochures which had brought people to the colonies. These still brought people to the new nation. Now there were lots of new legends—of rich land, undiscovered mines, and fast-growing cities. And there was the real-life romance of a new nation with its doors open and its people's eyes on the future.

When you had so little to lose, why not try America?

By now nearly fifty million people have crossed the oceans to settle in the United States. This is almost as large as the total number of people in Great Britain or France in our day.

It was lucky that the United States had so much unfilled land. The overflow of the Old World could find a place in the New. Peoples who did not know one another or who had fought against one another could now live side by side. America was called the "last best hope of mankind." The story of European hopelessness is a story of American hope.

In the years between the American Revolution and the Civil War, the two great sources of new Americans were Ireland and Germany. Events in those countries far across the Atlantic Ocean helped make the United States a world-nation.

In September 1845 a paper in Dublin, Ireland, gave its usual happy report of the harvest season. "The autumn is waning sunnily and cheerfully for the country. It is a busy and hopeful time. The husbandman is merrily at his toil, because it has rich promise; and the beautiful Giver of all good has, by a guarantee of abundance in the bad food of the poor, given assurance against famine."

Potatoes were the main food of the Irish poor.

One day the next month a young farmer in the north of Ireland said "he felt a peculiar smell. . . . It was the smell of the blight upon the potatoes." The terrible Irish famine was on its way. That year the blight spoiled a full third of the Irish potato crop. In 1846, the blight destroyed the whole crop all over the country. The potato blight continued until 1850.

"The hunger is upon us!" wailed the poor people of Ireland. Their misery, according to a Boston sea captain who visited Cork, was something "to harrow up your hearts." Everywhere was "the smell of the grave." A Quaker missionary found thousands on the northwest coast of Ireland "living or rather starving on turnip-tops, sand-eels, and sea-weed, a diet which no one in England would consider fit for the meanest animal which he keeps."

Tens of thousands died of starvation. Weakened by hunger, hundreds of thousands more died of disease. Typhus, relapsing fever (carried by ticks or lice), dysentery (from eating garbage), scurvy, and dozens of other ailments carried away many who did not die of hunger. Travelers reported that if you drove a cart down an Irish road at night and felt a bump, it was likely to be the dead body of a famine victim. Death haunted the land.

Ireland never was a rich country, and for centuries its produce had been drained off to England. Irish peasants were left just enough to keep them alive with strength enough to work the farms of the English. Most Irish peasants were Catholics, but the ruling British were Protestants and also persecuted them for their religion. The downtrodden Irish

The Irish famine, which drove families like this to desperate search for some shred of food, also prodded them to seek a new life in America. (London Illustrated News, 1849.)

tried to revolt time after time, but they were not able to throw off English rule. As the population of England grew, the English were more anxious than ever to have the Irish food for themselves.

Irishmen said, then, that Almighty God had sent the potato blight, but the English created the famine. Even while the poor of Ireland were dying of hunger for want of potatoes, there was food enough for the rich English landlords. Shiploads of wheat, oats, barley, flour, oatmeal, along with beef, pork, bacon, lard and butter that had been raised in Ireland, were sent across the narrow Irish Sea to feed the nearby people of England.

The poor people of Ireland were not even second-class citizens. They were more like slaves. Judges and sheriffs were Protestants. After 1829, when Britain passed a "Catholic Emancipation Act," the Catholics were still not really free. The theory was that now Catholics could vote. But woe to the Irishman who voted against the English landlord!

Again and again the desperate peasants organized for rebellion. They organized secret societies (some called themselves "Whiteboys," others "Terry Alts," "Hearts of Steel," or "Molly Maguires") to terrorize the worst landlords. But they made little headway. By the time of the Irish famine in 1845, the peasants of Ireland were still little better than slaves.

Even before the famine, Irish had been coming to America by the thousands. America, in the phrase of the time, was "a sort of half-way stage to Heaven." To many Irish it seemed almost as hard to get here as to reach heaven, because the cost of a steerage ticket across the ocean (between $12.50 and $25.00) seemed so high. Letters written back to Ireland made everybody want to come. "This is the best country in the world," wrote one Irish girl from New York City in 1848. "It is easy making money in this country but hard to save it." One new arrival wrote back with glee that the Irish here "eat the pig themselves, and have plenty of bread to their potatoes." "Every day is like a Christmas Day for meat."

And now the Irish came by the hundreds of thousands. Through the port of New York City alone, between 1847 and 1860, from Ireland there came over a million. That was nearly half of all the Europeans who landed in New York in those years.

But once the Irish had landed in Boston or New York or some other port city, they had very little choice about where to go. Few had the money to move on. And few wanted to move to a lonely Western farm. The farming they knew in Ireland did not make them lovers of the land.

Many of those who moved westward in the early years used their strong arms and sturdy backs to dig canals and build railroads. The Erie Canal was a ditch 363 miles long, 40 feet wide, and 4 feet deep. It ran from Albany on the Hudson River to Buffalo on Lake Erie, and connected the growing West to New York City. When the digging began in 1817, there were not many Irish around, but before it was completed eight years later, the Irish were arriving by the thousands. On the canal they had a reputation for strength, courage, and willingness to work. Irish contractors organized teams

The Erie Canal in 1831.

of their fellow immigrants.

When the Erie Canal was finished in 1825, they moved on to help build other canals and then the railroads, which brought life to many instant cities. Soon people could say that "of the several sorts of power working at the fabric of the Republic—water-power, steam-power, and Irish-power," Irish-power had worked the hardest.

Those who stayed in the cities along the Atlantic were not always welcomed. In places like Boston they were kept out of the best jobs. Advertisements often ended: "No Irish Need Apply." The bewildered new arrivals needed help, and they received it mostly from Irishmen who had come before them. The Irish liked the sociable city life. They found a new use for what they had learned in Ireland while organizing secret clubs to fight unfair laws and English landlords. Democracy gave them their chance. Now, in New York City and Boston, they banded together to elect Irish aldermen to the city government.

The Irish alderman could help provide government jobs and money and advice. If a new arrival was arrested for a petty crime, the alderman helped him find a lawyer, or persuaded the judge to let him off. The alderman organized benefit dances. The money people paid for dance tickets would go to some Irish worker who had been crippled at his work, or to an Irish widow who had no way of supporting her children. The alderman found doctors for the sick, and brought groceries to the poor. He reached into his pocket to give a few dollars to needy orphans, or to men wanting a new start in business. He was a one-man Community Chest. No wonder the Irish in the Sixth Ward in New York City voted again and again for Dennis McCarthy (who had been a liquor dealer) or Thomas S. Brady (a lawyer) or Felix O'Neill (a grocer).

These men had a clear and simple idea of what politics was for. It was to help the needy Irish who had voted for them. They were not "statesmen." Sometimes they were not too honest, and

kept a good share for themselves. But they had warm hearts and helped other newly arrived fellow Americans who had nowhere else to turn.

The Irish loved politics. They were good at it, and they loved the growing cities where they found their chance to be politicians. Their old Irish experience in the Whiteboys, the Terry Alts, and the Molly Maguires—when they had terrorized the tyrannic English—

The welcome to some Irish and German immigrants was a modern version of what the earliest settlers received from unfriendly Indians. Here we see a recent immigrant in Baltimore terrorized by members of a secret society who, because they refused to answer questions about themselves, were called "Know-Nothings."

was now a great help. In Boston and New York and other cities, if all other arguments failed, they were not afraid to use their fists.

Mike Walsh had been born in Ireland, and was brought here as a child. Wandering the streets of New York as a runaway apprentice, he learned the ways of the poor. In 1840 he organized his "Spartan Band" to take over the city's Democratic Party from an old political club which called itself "Tammany Hall." His Spartan Band was really a gang. They went into meetings, using fists instead of votes to defeat their enemies.

Walsh called his newspaper *The Subterranean*. It stood for the "subterranean democracy"—that is, the people who were underground or downtrodden. His motto was "Independent in Everything —Neutral in Nothing." He had a sense of humor. As a Congressman he made fun of stupid and wasteful projects by proposing to build a lighthouse on the Erie Canal. He liked to orate and knew how to stir up an audience. "I will yet ride over all this rotten opposition," he said, "like a balloon over a dunghill!"

Prizefighting was against the law but the Irish took the lead. One of their heroes was John "Old Smoke" Morrissey. He got his nickname during a barroom fight when a stove which had been knocked over set fire to his coattails. "Old Smoke" rose from the burning coals, and with his coattails flaming he scored a knockout. In 1853, when he was only twenty-two years old, he won the heavyweight championship from "Yankee" Sullivan in a fight that lasted thirty-seven rounds. Morrissey

was sometimes called the Irish Strong Boy.

In those days the fighters wore no gloves, but fought with bare knuckles. There were almost no rules, and fights went on as long as necessary, some lasting more than a hundred rounds. The Irish were the pioneers of prizefighting. After horse racing, it was the first important American spectator sport.

America, then, offered all sorts of new opportunities. People had a chance to discover that they could do new things. An Irish peasant, beaten down in the old country, here might become a prizefighter hero, or might help build canals and railroads, or might organize the government of cities.

The other large group of new arrivals in the years before the Civil War was the Germans. Nobody planned it that way, but whenever and wherever the people of Europe suffered, the United States somehow gained. Over there, 1816 was the terrible "year without a summer." Hail and sleet fell at all seasons. The Rhine River flooded, floating away barns and livestock. Autumn storms uprooted fruit trees. Hunger and misery cursed the land. We cannot be surprised, then, that during the following year about eight thousand Germans arrived in American ports. Again in 1829–30, the winter was one of the worst in the history of Europe. People froze because there was not enough wood to burn in fireplaces. Food was scarcer than ever, and prices went up.

By 1832, more than ten thousand Germans were coming to America in a single year. As suffering on the German countryside deepened, it became plain that

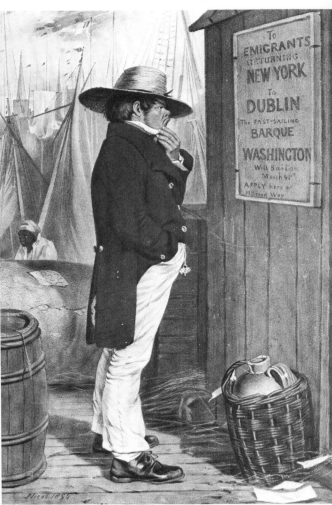

An Irishman who left home as a pauper (left) could hope to return as a rich man.

their governments were not going to help. Then Germans started coming to America by the tens of thousands. They continued to come in vast numbers till nearly the end of the nineteenth century. In 1854 alone (when Germans were half of all immigrants to the United States) they numbered nearly a quarter-million. The move to America became a craze. One night people would decide to leave Germany and they would leave the next morning. A thirteen-year-old boy with a pack on his back walked the three hundred miles to the French port of Le Havre in order to find passage for America.

Throughout these years, revolutions were brewing in Germany. Students formed secret societies and studied new constitutions, hoping to overthrow the government. Peasants gathered around "Liberty Trees." They refused to pay taxes and roughed up tax officials.

In Central Europe, Prince Metternich, the enemy of democracy, was in charge. He had seen the terror of the French Revolution of 1789, and he hated democracy, which he imagined was always government by a mob. He organized tyranny in Germany. But even Metternich could not prevent protests like that in May 1832 when 25,000 people gathered in a small German town to drink the health of Lafayette (the hero of the American Revolution) and to demand a republic.

Metternich's policies created a growing flood of refugees. By 1848, there was civil war and a full-fledged revolution in Germany. The country was in turmoil, and many revolutionaries had to flee.

These political refugees from Germany were not many—perhaps only a few thousand. But they included some, like Carl Schurz, who became eminent here and helped to build in America the democracy they could not build in Germany. When the German Revolution failed in 1852, Schurz came to the United States. His career covered the whole country. After becoming a lawyer in Milwaukee, he campaigned for Lincoln in 1860, fought as a general on the Northern side at Gettysburg and other battles. He was Minister to Spain, Senator from Missouri, and then served in the Cabinet as Secretary of the Interior. He was one of the leading Americans of his day.

Germany's loss was America's gain. New Americans from Germany built whole cities like Milwaukee, and helped make Milwaukee a center of American beer brewing. They spread all over the country, becoming farmers, teachers, professors, lawyers, doctors, newspapermen, and they built prosperous businesses. Many fought on the Union side in the Civil War.

The German passion for music showed in folk-singing clubs and in new symphony orchestras. The orchestra in Chicago was directed and manned by Germans for many years. They helped found American colleges and universities. The Germans brought with them some new ideas about schools. They believed in physical education and many early physical education teachers were German. They persuaded Americans to build gymnasiums attached to schools. Before the Germans came, it was not usual to send children to school before they were old enough to read. Then Germans brought over the *Kindergarten* (a German word meaning "garden of children") where children as young as four years old could learn by playing. The idea caught on, and soon there were American kindergartens everywhere.

In the half-century before the Civil War, although the largest numbers came from Germany and Ireland, immigrants

---

Instant Americans. Old friends talk German to an immigrant girl two weeks after her arrival from Germany. "You are mistaken," she replies haughtily. "I don't speak German."

were coming from other places, too. Thousands came from the Scandinavian countries, from the Netherlands, Belgium, Switzerland, France, and elsewhere. The nation was growing by a great migration.

CHAPTER 16

Instant Cities

In places where men still alive could remember the sound of the Indian war whoop and the shadow of the virgin forest, there sprouted cities.

On riverways and the joinings of riverways appeared Pittsburgh, Cincinnati, St. Louis, Louisville, Memphis, Minneapolis and St. Paul, Davenport, Des Moines, Omaha, and hundreds of others. On the Great Lakes and at the river entrances to the Lakes, men founded Rochester, Buffalo, Cleveland, Toledo, Detroit, and Chicago. Around the river entrances to the Gulf Coast appeared Mobile, Galveston, and Houston, in addition, of course, to New Orleans. And now on the far Pacific shores there were Portland, Seattle, San Francisco, and Los Angeles. An astonishing crop of cities to grow so quickly across a wilderness-continent!

When before had so many cities grown so fast? In America the moving spirit was in the air. In England or France, where families had lived in the same village for centuries, it took a lot of spunk to leave the old homestead and move to a new place. But over here were the children and grandchildren of people who had come from Europe, three thousand miles across an ocean. They did not think it so odd that they too should move on. Americans easily took root in new places.

In the years between the Revolution and the Civil War, Americans went west to start new cities. Many hoped to make their living out of building them. Some hoped to make money out of selling the land. The wilderness was worth very little, but once a city was there, land became valuable. Then some people would want to buy land for houses, others for farms to raise vegetables and chickens and eggs nearby where there would be no problem of transportation.

Merchants came to open their stores. New towns were good for young doctors in search of patients, and for young lawyers looking for clients. Even if you were inexperienced and unknown, you could still get started, because everybody else there was also unknown. You did not have to take business away from old established firms, because there were none. But the value of your land and your business, whatever it was, depended on more people coming.

This was when the American businessman began. About 1830 in these new Western cities, the word "businessman" took a meaning it had never had before. A businessman was not just a merchant, trying to sell people something from his store. He was a man who had staked his living on a new town. He expected great

Big-city politicians provided useful services for new immigrants. Here, a magazine artist of 1856 shows members of New York's Tammany Hall helping immigrants from Europe, Africa, and Asia to become naturalized as American citizens. On election day these politicians expected the new citizens to remember their friends.

things, and tried his hand at all sorts of new enterprises. He prospered only when the town prospered. Naturally he was cheerful about the future.

The great cities of the Old World had been built on their rich past. To satisfy the many people who were already there, citizens had provided one thing after another—a newspaper to give them news, inns to house the travelers, theaters and opera houses to entertain the crowds, colleges and universities where the learned men could gather and the young could be educated. A European city grew up piece by piece, over decades and centuries. An older city had more to offer simply because it was older. Over there the people had come first, and then the city was slowly built to meet their needs. This seemed an obvious and sensible way for a city to grow.

But that way was much too slow and haphazard for impatient, purposeful Americans. Western city-builders wanted their city first. They wanted to see it even *before* the people were there. If they already had a newspaper, hotel, theater, and college or university, then surely people would come. But if they waited, then some other city might provide all those attractions first. People would then go on to Cleveland instead of staying in Pittsburgh, or they would

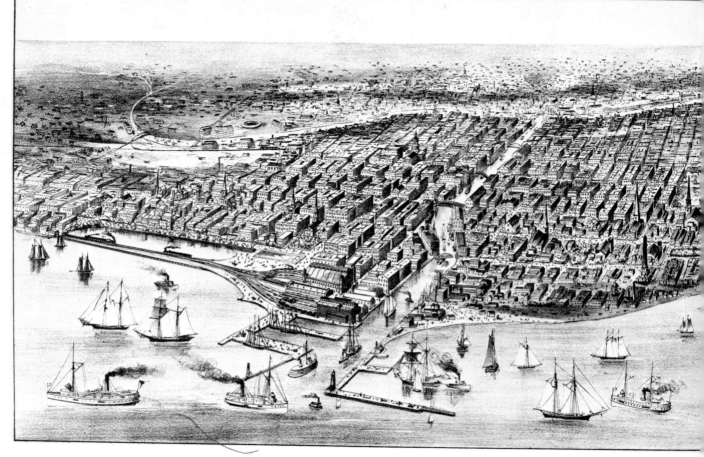

move on from Kansas City to Omaha, or from Omaha to Denver.

The men who went west in the early nineteenth century were often going to cities that did not yet really exist. To them a city was not just any place where lots of people happened to live. It was where people were building a community together. They built not for their needs but for their hopes.

For example, in Europe a city did not have a newspaper until it already had a large reading community. But in the American West, the newspaper actually arrived *before* the city. Your place might never even become a city unless you *started* with a newspaper.

To men of the Old World, it seemed foolish to start a newspaper in the wilderness. But Americans had strong imaginations. They imagined their great cities—Pittsburgh, Cleveland, Chicago, Kansas City—sprouting in the backwoods. To make their dreams come true, they first needed a newspaper. "The spirit of adventure," a pioneer St. Louis editor boasted, "thrust it forward ahead of the calaboose, the post office, the school, the church, and made it a symbol of conquest." Along with the axe and the musket, the newspaper press became a way of subduing the wilderness. Here was a new kind of pioneer—the

---

Chicago was one of the most spectacular of the instant cities. Top: Chicago as a tiny settlement in 1820. Bottom: By about 1860 Chicago had become a thriving metropolis of more than 100,000 people. This is a print from the firm of Currier and Ives, whose scenes of American life were popular in the nineteenth century.

newspaper-pioneer.

Along the Atlantic Coast in older American cities, newspapers had been more like those in England. They satisfied people who were already there. But in the new Western cities, at first newspapers were advertisements. Like the early colonial advertising brochures for Georgia and the other colonies, they aimed to attract people. Then their place would become as great as the writers pretended it already was.

Pittsburgh, west of the Alleghenies, was a tiny village with a population of only three hundred when the Pittsburgh *Gazette,* its first newspaper, appeared on July 29, 1786. A small press, together with type, ink, and paper, had been packed across the mountains. It was hard to get supplies. Once, when the outfit ran out of paper, they borrowed from Fort Pitt some cartridge paper that was supposed to be used for wrapping ammunition. Since there was no mail service, the editor delivered the papers himself, while at the same time he gathered news for the next issue. The main purpose of the newspaper was to advertise Pittsburgh and attract settlers there.

John Scull, who started that first Pittsburgh newspaper even before there was a city, became a leader of the city when it actually appeared. He became postmaster, president of a bank, a founder of the new University of Pittsburgh, and a member of the town council. Before Scull died in 1828, Pittsburgh was a thriving city of twelve thousand.

This same success story could be told again and again. To succeed with your newspaper, you had to be able to do many different things. It was not enough to be able to write. You had to be able to collect the news, to set the type, and then be willing yourself to do all sorts of chores, like delivering the paper.

There were many "Franklins of the West" who used their printing presses to build their cities. But there were risks. In the little village of Cincinnati (with a population of less than four hundred), when the first newspaper, called the *Centinel of the Northwestern Territory*, appeared in 1793 it warned of house burning and massacre by Indians. A "Public Notice" in that paper offered a government reward of $168 for "every scalp, having the right ear appendant, for the first ten Indians" killed in the neighborhood.

By the middle of the nineteenth century there were cheap portable printing presses. One, called the "army press," was only a foot across and could be lifted by one man. With $150 you could set yourself up as a newspaperman. But you had to be energetic and willing to move around till you found the right place.

Young Robert Thompson Van Horn, who was destined to be the newspaper-pioneer of Kansas City, showed how to do it. Born in Pennsylvania in 1824, he tried his hand at teaching school and at being a lawyer. Then moving westward, he edited several papers. Everywhere he went his newspaper advertised some new city which still had to be built. "Standing around scratching heads," his newspaper warned an Ohio village in 1850, "will never make Pomeroy the city nature intended it to be." Disappointed with Pomeroy, he moved on to Cincinnati. When his printing plant there burned down, he took a job on a river steamboat.

"I am going out West, probably to Nebraska," Van Horn wrote his parents in 1854, "where I hope to retrieve my fortunes and kick up a dust generally among the natives." When he was working in St. Louis, a committee of businessmen from Kansas City went to ask him to come edit their newspaper. He took up their offer. Beginning with only $250 he became Kansas City's pioneer newspaperman.

The main problems of these newspaper-pioneers, one of them explained,

A hazard of journalism in the West. A reader "requests" a retraction of an uncomplimentary statement. This editor, like many others, also acted as postmaster. This gave him an opportunity—not quite legal —to gather news from incoming letters before they were delivered.

were "to get paper, to get news, and to get paid." Cash was scarce, and editors had to be willing to be paid in produce. They even advertised that you could pay them in corn, molasses, potatoes, cabbage, flour, meal, fruit, or kindling wood. One editor announced that he would accept "any other variety of produce except babies."

In 1846, foreign travelers to western Tennessee, along the banks of the Mississippi River, were astonished to find there in a remote forest in the middle of nowhere a large and imposing hotel. Fronted by an elegant facade of tall white columns, it called itself the "Gayoso House." It was still three years before Memphis would be incorporated as a city, and ten years before there would be a railroad. Where were the guests? In the future, of course. The men who built the hotel expected the guests to come quickly enough. They were sure that Memphis would soon become a great city. *First* it needed a "spacious and elegant hotel." To Europeans, this seemed all topsy-turvy.

When the English novelist Anthony Trollope traveled across America in the 1860's, he noted:

Hotels in America are very much larger and more numerous than in other countries. They are to be found in all towns, and I might almost say in all villages. In England and on the Continent we find them on the recognized routes of travel and in towns of commercial or social importance. . . . But in the States of Amer-

---

An early passenger elevator of the kind first used in hotels.

ica, the first sign of . . . settlement is an hotel five stories high with an office, a bar, a cloak-room, three gentlemen's parlours, two ladies' parlours, a ladies' entrance and two hundred bedrooms. . . .

Whence are to come the sleepers in those two hundred bedrooms, and who is to pay for the gaudy sofas and numerous lounging chairs in the ladies' parlours? . . . When the new hotel rises up in the wilderness, it is presumed that people will come there with the express object of inhabiting it. The hotel itself will create a population, — as the railways do. With us [in Europe] railways run to the towns; but in the States the towns run to the railways. It is the same thing with the hotels.

Nearly everything about the American hotel was new. Even the word was new to the English language. "Hotel" was borrowed from the French language, where it meant a noble house or a city hall. The old English "inn" was a modest building with a few rooms where tired travelers could sleep. In England, "tavern" was the name for the place where you could get food or drink. The American "hotel" combined the services of the inn and the tavern.

The architecture was new. The American hotel was often the biggest and most imposing building in the wilderness place that hoped to become a city. It looked less like a modest English inn than like a great church or a palace. The St. Charles Hotel in New Orleans struck English visitors in 1846 by its "large and elegant Corinthian portico and the lofty swelling dome." American hotels were impressive public buildings. They came to be called "Palaces of the Public" or "People's Palaces." And they deserved the name. For they were the social centers where a democratic people could meet, just as European nobles had met in the lobbies and courtyards of their ruling princes.

Hotels were where all sorts of conveniences were first tried. Some of the first systems of central heating were in hotels. A furnace blew hot air through the public rooms so that visitors did not have to rely on a fireplace. The first public building in America heated by steam was the Eastern Exchange Hotel in Boston (1846). But it was a long while before it seemed worth the trouble to heat the bedrooms.

The Tremont House in Boston was probably the first large building in modern times to have extensive plumbing. One of its most famous features was a row of eight flush toilets (then called "water closets"). The bathtubs in the basement actually had running water, a curiosity at the time. In the Astor House, built in New York City in 1836, guests were astonished to find plumbing on the upper floors. Each floor had its own water closets and its own bathrooms, fed from a roof tank to which water had been raised by a steam pump.

The first passenger elevators (originally called "vertical railways") appeared in hotels. A passenger elevator was installed in the Fifth Avenue Hotel in New York in 1859. Until then the rooms on upper floors had been much cheaper. Who wanted to climb five or six flights of stairs? But when rooms on the top floor could be reached by an elevator, they actually had a special attraction. From a top-floor room, as one traveler suggested, a guest could "look down on surrounding buildings in the same manner as our most gracious English nobility look down on the peasants beneath them."

During a night in the city hotel many people became acquainted with conveniences which they then wanted for their own homes. Beds with springs were found in hotels long before people had them at home. People were still using oil lamps to light their homes when Boston's Tremont House in 1829 set a bright example with gas light in its public rooms. The Astor House in New York actually had its own gas plant.

It was in hotels that electricity was first used for bells and buzzers. Until then, when you wanted service in your room you shook a hand bell, incidentally waking up the other guests. One guest explained how the system worked: "One ring for ice-water, two for bell-boy, three for porter, four for chambermaid,—and not a darned one of them will come."

By the time of the Civil War, the hotels of the United States were already famous throughout the world. "The American hotel," a London newspaperman reported in 1861, "is to an English hotel what an elephant is to a periwinkle. . . . An American hotel is (in the chief cities) as roomy as Buckingham Palace, and is not much inferior to a palace in its internal fittings." When an English comedian stayed at the luxurious St. Nicholas Hotel in New York he was reminded of the Arabian Nights. He was afraid, he said, to leave his shoes outside the door to be shined (as was the custom in Europe) for fear someone would cover them with gold.

Hotels drew people together and became the centers of social life in the new Western cities. There the rich gave their parties. The lobby was the meeting place

Brown's Indian Queen Hotel, Washington, D.C., about 1832. This elegant building stood on Pennsylvania Avenue, about midway between the Capitol and the White House.

The expanding West: dream and nightmare. Unscrupulous land promoters were described by Charles Dickens in Martin Chuzzlewit *after his 1842 tour of the United States.* Left: *"The thriving City of Eden, as it appeared on paper."* Right: *"The thriving City of Eden, as it appeared in fact."* (Illustrations by Phiz.)

of leading citizens. Since Americans moved so freely around the country many who could afford it lived in hotels —until their own houses could be built, or until they decided where to settle. An American city was judged not by its cathedrals or by its government buildings, but by its hotels.

Yet it was risky business trying to build an instant city. We remember the successes, but there were many more failures. These became ghost towns. When we drive through the West today, we can see what is left of a few of them. Some, like the abandoned silver-mining towns of Aspen and Central City, Colorado, have been revived as curiosities, to serve for skiing resorts in winter and tourist centers for summer opera.

Most ghost towns have left no trace. When the mines ran out, or when neigh-boring farmers found the land would not grow crops, or when there was a drought, or when the hoped-for canal or railroad did not come, citizens left for some other, more promising town. We can never know exactly how many there were of these "melancholy deserted villages, monuments of blighted hopes." But there were thousands. In Iowa alone, between 1838 (when Iowa became a territory) and the early twentieth century, we can count over twenty-two hundred abandoned places. In Kansas there were even more than that number of ghost towns—towns whose people had walked away in the last half of the nineteenth century.

Sometimes, when people realized that a village would never become a city, they would actually take down the buildings to use the lumber in some other place where they had moved their hopes. Sometimes, when the people finally gave up, their town was already (in a Kansas phrase) "too dead to skin."

The glory of American cities was always in the future. Visitors from England were sometimes puzzled by the American language. Americans tended to confuse what had already happened with what they simply expected to happen. In England the word "city" had a very precise meaning. It was used only for a large and impressive place. A smaller place was called a "town," a "village," or a "hamlet." In England a city meant a place big enough to have a cathedral, which was the headquarters of a bishop. Englishmen would not call a place a city unless it was old and thriving, with thousands of people.

Americans, though, looked ahead. They were so certain that their places in the wilderness would quickly become cities that they did not bother to wait. They preferred to call them cities right now. Then by a kind of magic, they thought, the name would attract people and help make the place become a real city. This amused foreign travelers. "In the course of the last two days," the Earl of Derby reported in 1826, "we passed several *cities*—some of them however almost invisible."

"It is strange that the name of city should be given to an unfinished loghouse," the English Captain Marryat noted in 1834, "but such is the case in Texas!"

CHAPTER 17
Every Man His Own Carpenter

In their instant cities Americans needed houses. And they needed them quickly. There were no grandparents or other relatives to live with until you had a home of your own. There were no old houses to rent or to buy. And out in the West carpenters were scarce, or nonexistent. If you wanted shelter you had to provide it yourself.

Americans, then, invented a new way of building. The novel idea was very simple.

In England, builders of houses had got into a rut. They believed there was only one right way to build a wooden house. You built it around a frame of heavy timbers. Each timber was about

a foot square. You held these heavy timbers together by cutting down the end of one into a tongue (a "tenon") which was then fitted into a hole (a "mortise") in the adjoining timber. When there was a pull on the joint you held the pieces together with a wooden peg

The old style of house building required that at each joint a "tenon" be carved so it would exactly fit into its "mortise." A wooden peg was inserted to hold the tenon in place.

Before the balloon-frame house was invented, the framework of a house was made of heavy timbers which might first be put together on the ground. Then a crew of men was needed to lift the cumbersome sections.

fitted into a hole that went through both the joined timbers. You rested your floors on these heavy supports, and closed in the sides with mud, plaster, or wood.

There were advantages to this kind of building. The weighty frame was not easily shaken or moved. But to make it required lots of skill. You had to be an experienced carpenter, clever with the crude tools of the day, to make mortise-and-tenon joints that fit tight. It took lots of time to square off the huge, cumbersome timbers and to carve the joints just right. In new Western towns like Cincinnati, Chicago, Omaha, and Denver, where carpenters were not to be found, the people themselves did not have the skill—much less the time—to build their own houses in the old style.

All these needs produced the "balloon frame." Nobody knows exactly who invented this new American type of building. But we do know that it began to appear in the Western instant cities. Probably the first was built in Chicago in 1833. The name "balloon-frame house" was used by respectable, old-fashioned builders because they thought the whole building was ridiculously light. The first wind, they said, would surely blow it away—just like a balloon. They could not believe that anything as quick and as light as the new Chicago construction could possibly hold up.

What was the balloon frame? The idea

is so simple that it is hard to believe it ever had to be invented. The first notion was to forget that you ever needed a frame of heavy timbers with their ends neatly carved to fit into one another. Instead make the lightest possible frame! Get a supply of long thin boards about two inches thick and four inches wide. Then buy some long heavy nails. Stand up some of the thin boards—say eighteen inches or two feet apart—and nail other thin boards across them to hold them together.

Once you have your frame up, cover it outside and in with thin wide clapboards or any other material you wish. Nothing could be simpler. About three-quarters of the wooden houses in the United States are now built this way.

Of course, to build a balloon frame you need plenty of nails. In the old days, nails had been extremely expensive, because each one was fashioned by hand. But by 1830 New England nail-making machines were turning out nails by the thousands, better and cheaper than before.

Anybody could build a balloon-frame

The construction of a balloon-frame house in 1855. The light boards of the frame are simply held together by nails.

house. You only had to be able to use a hammer. "To erect a balloon-building," someone explained in 1855, "requires about as much mechanical skill as it does to build a board fence." Clever carpenters and builders experienced in the old ways naturally could not believe that a sturdy house could be so simple to build.

The new way of building was speedy. It took less than half the time to build a balloon-frame house than one of the same size built in the old style. In Chicago, within one week in April, 1834, seven new buildings of this kind appeared. By mid-June there were seventy-five more. By October an additional five hundred were in use.

The balloon frame proved to have other advantages that nobody had counted on. It turned out to be even stronger and more durable than the old heavy-timbered construction. For moisture had tended to collect in the joints where the old heavy timbers were fitted together. Then the timbers would begin to rot. The beams were also weakened by the holes cut for tenons and drilled for wooden pegs. On the other hand, the balloon frame, which used lots of thin boards, did not weaken them with holes. It used the whole plank and the very grain of the wood so as to stand the most strain.

For Americans on the move, the balloon frame had still another great advantage. It could be taken apart easily and then set up again in some other place. The old heavy-timbered buildings had been made to stay forever in the same place. But the boards of a balloon frame were light and easy to carry. St. Mary's Church in Chicago, said to be the first balloon-frame building, within ten years of its construction was taken down, moved away, and reerected three times.

Ambitious Americans, always on the lookout for better opportunities in another place, might want to take their houses with them. In Omaha, General William Larimer in 1856 was living in a balloon-frame house that had first been set up in Pittsburgh, then knocked down and shipped out west by steamboat. When Omaha grew, he moved his house to another site.

As balloon-frame houses became popular and the demand increased, companies manufactured and sold them in large quantities. You could order your house from a catalog by mail, and the nails and the boards (cut to the right size) would be shipped out to you with some simple directions. You could put up your house, then, wherever you pleased, with the help of a few friends. By 1850, in New York alone, about five thousand such prefabs were being made to send out to relieve the housing shortage among Gold Rushers in California. One company shipped 100 portable wooden houses which were carried on pack mules across the Isthmus of Panama; another sent out 175 all the way by sea around Cape Horn.

Not only houses, but also churches and even hotels were commonly built with ready-made balloon frames. The spacious San Francisco Astor House, a three-and-a-half-story hotel 180 feet long, containing ten shops and a hundred rooms, was erected from a kit ordered by Westerners who needed shelter in a hurry.

PART FOUR

THINKING LIKE
AMERICANS

Americans were united by the new experiences they were sharing every day. By the time of the Civil War, there were clearly recognizable American ways of life and American ways of thinking. Americans devised new ways of making things—not only houses, but muskets and locks and clocks and nearly everything else. Americans, too, became more like one another simply because they had to do more things for themselves. In Europe many of their tasks would have been done for them by professionals, with their own ancient royal guilds and monopolies.

Americans were pushed together because, to cross the continent safely, they had to leave behind many of their belongings—together with old prejudices and snobberies. They learned to act more equal and more friendly.

Out of all this, too, grew new American kinds of political parties. In this new world, politics was not just for the few. The American party conventions became a popular entertainment, and election campaigns became a national circus with as many different circus rings as there were States.

The citizens of the new nation had begun thinking like Americans. Not so much because they were trying—but mostly because they could not help it. Living like Americans was what made Americans.

Here was being created a "nation of nations." Americans were united less by memories than by hopes, less by a shared past than by an exciting present and by dreams of the future.

CHAPTER 18

American Know-how

Back in January 1801, the American people were frightened. The French dictator Napoleon seemed out to conquer the world. He had overrun Egypt, as a step toward taking India away from the British Empire. He invaded Syria on the far edge of the Holy Land. In the opening year of the new century, he sent his troops in winter across the snowy Swiss Alps to occupy Milan. And now he was on his way to conquering Italy. After defeating the Austrians in a great battle at Hohenlinden he was master of Central Europe. He had even forced the Spanish to give him the vast American territory called Louisiana.

Americans yet had no inkling of the surprising events that were to make Louisiana part of the United States. Napoleon still seemed unbeatable. Would the United States be his next victim?

John Adams of Massachusetts, who was President, warned the country that it was no use trying to talk Napoleon out of his adventures. The new nation, young and weak, had to prepare for a French attack. America needed guns. And the worst of it was that America had very few gun-makers. There was still no such thing as a gun factory anywhere in the world, much less in primitive America. The muskets Americans had used in the Revolution twenty years before had come from France or elsewhere in Europe. Now, to keep the United States safe, guns had to be made within the country. There was no time to waste.

In those days in Europe a whole musket was made by one man. He was called a "gunsmith." (The word "smith" came from an older word meaning to shape or cut.) Just as a goldsmith shaped pieces of gold into jewelry, so the gunsmith actually shaped all the pieces of a gun to make them fit together. It seemed obvious, then, that unless the United States could import lots of gunsmiths, it would not have the guns it needed.

An American named Eli Whitney refused to see it that way. Whitney had a notion that there might be an entirely new way of making muskets. Born on a farm in Massachusetts, as a boy he had puttered around his father's machine shop, where he learned to use a mechanic's tools. He was so clever with his hands that he could make and repair violins. By the time he was fifteen years old he had hired helpers for his own business of manufacturing nails. Later he made hatpins.

At the age of twenty-three, he decided that he needed a college education after all. When he entered Yale College in 1789, he was eight years older than his classmates. After he graduated in 1792, he went down south to live with the family of the Revolutionary General Nathanael Greene, on their plantation outside Savannah, Georgia.

It was easy to grow cotton on plantations in the South. But there was no easy way of separating the fuzz attached to the cotton seeds from the seeds themselves. The cotton fuzz had to be separated so it could be twisted into cotton threads. In those days the seeds had to be taken out by hand one at a time. It was so much trouble that cotton was not a very valuable crop. When people in the neighborhood saw that Whitney was clever at repairing things about the plantation, they asked him to set his mind to making a machine to solve their great problem. And within ten days he had actually made a "cotton gin." ("Gin" was short for "engine.") His was an extremely simple machine. The worker turned a crank attached to combs that combed out the fuzz from the seeds. Now one man could clean fifty pounds of cotton in a day.

Suddenly cotton became a valuable crop. The South soon exported large

A cotton gin.

quantities of cotton up north and all over the world. In 1794, within two years after Whitney's invention, the South was exporting a million and a half pounds of cotton, the next year over six million pounds, and by 1800 cotton exports from the South reached nearly eighteen million pounds.

Whitney, without intending to, had changed the life of the South. But now the whole nation was in desperate need. Could he find a way of making guns without gunsmiths?

His idea again was very simple. Each musket was made of fifty different parts. For one man to make all these parts himself he had to be a skillful gunsmith, and had to know a great deal about guns. But suppose a man had to make only *one* of these parts. Suppose you gave the man a model of that one part and invented for him the right tools so he could quickly make lots of precise copies. That might be as simple as tracing out copies of a paper doll. Instead of tracing on paper, he would trace on sheets of iron. The man would not need much skill at all. You could quickly show him how to make a hundred copies of that one part in a single day. Then suppose you found forty-nine other men and trained each man to make lots of copies of another one of the parts.

When all the men had finished their day's work, you would have a hundred copies of each of the different parts in a musket. Of course you would have to be very careful about your measurements. But if you could make each copy exactly like every other copy of the same part, then any one part would fit together with any other. It would be easy to put the fifty parts of the musket together.

In this way you would have done a kind of magic. You would have made guns without a single skilled gunsmith! If your copy-making machinery was good, you could even make the guns much faster.

This was a neat trick. It was Eli Whitney's idea for supplying the nation's guns. But very few people believed it would work. It was too hard to imagine that good guns could be made without gunsmiths. Of course the leading "experts" on the question were the few gunsmiths in the United States at that time. They were harder to convince than anybody else. When the Secretary of War asked them whether Whitney's plan would work, they simply laughed. Whitney thought the best answer was a demonstration.

In the wintry January of 1801, Eli Whitney came to Washington for the climax of his years of work and planning. Three years before, in January 1798, when he had first begun to figure out his new plan, he had promised the government to make ten thousand muskets. That was a fantastic number. Whitney was not a gunsmith and had never made even one gun before. When he promised to make guns for the government, he had not even seen the gun he was going to make. Was the Secretary of War crazy to put the arming of the nation in the hands of an amateur?

But Whitney had faith in his new kind of mechanical magic. What he had in his mind was not simply a new way of making guns. It was a new way of making *anything!*

His idea was so new that the machinery for it did not yet exist. Before he could make any muskets in his new way, he had to make the machinery for making the muskets. He spent over two years inventing and perfecting the tools that would make precise iron copies of the single part which was used as a pattern. He made new kinds of measuring machines so the worker could be sure his part was precisely the right size. Since he had spent so much time making the new machinery, he had been able to make very few muskets. Even his friends began to wonder whether his system was only a pipe dream. Would it work at all?

Now he had a chance to show. He had an appointment with President John Adams, Vice-President Thomas Jefferson, the Secretary of War, the Secretary of the Treasury, and other members of the Cabinet. When they met he showed them one of his completed muskets. Then he laid out separate piles of the loose pieces. He told each man present to take one piece—any piece—from each pile and see how easily they all fitted together into a complete, working musket. They were astonished. Any one of the pieces actually fitted with all the others.

"He had invented," Jefferson reported, "moulds and machines for making all the pieces of his [flint]lock so exactly equal, that take 100 locks to pieces and mingle their parts and the hundred locks may be put together as well by taking the first pieces which come to hand . . . good locks may be put together without employing a [gun]smith."

The witnesses now had a new faith in Whitney and in his system. Not until 1809, ten years after Whitney began his assignment, did he finally deliver the last of the ten thousand muskets. For his work during all those years he made a profit of only $2,500. By then the United States had bought Louisiana and felt safer in the West. The menace of Napoleon was no longer so great. But the British were a new threat. They blocked American ships and seized American sailors. The United States might have to fight a second war for independence. Now the nation needed arms more than ever. Whitney was ready to help arm the nation.

Whitney's system soon was called the "Uniformity System"—because each part in one gun was uniform (precisely the same in shape and size) with that same part in another gun of the same design. Some called it the "Interchangeable System," because the parts of one gun were interchangeable with the parts from another.

The need for Whitney's system came from America's lack of skill. If we had had lots of trained gunsmiths here, he might never have thought of it. Yet to make his system work at all, his guns actually had to be better than those made altogether by an individual gunsmith. The parts from one gun would not fit another unless they were very precisely made. Whitney's enemies were surprised to find his guns even better than the imported guns made by trained craftsmen.

There were other advantages. In the old days, when a piece of your musket broke, you could not simply buy a new piece to put in its place. You had to take the whole musket to a gunsmith. He had

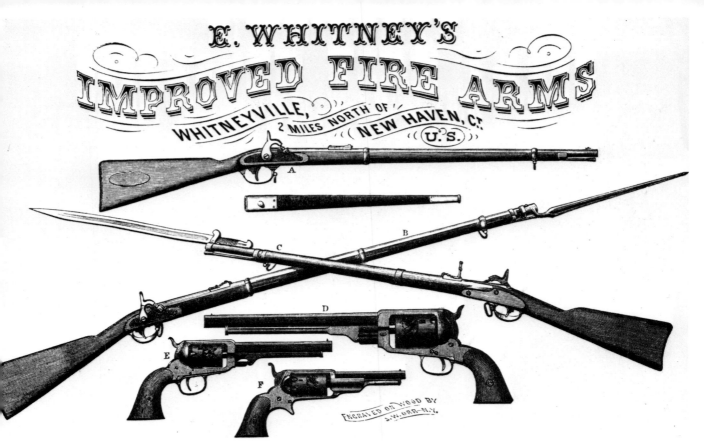

The "Uniformity System," turning out guns by the thousands, created the need and the opportunity for national advertising. This advertisement (about 1860) included a testimonial by the famous mountain man Kit Carson: "Whitney's Rifles are the best to cross the Plains with."

---

to manufacture a particular piece to fit that particular musket. Under the new Uniformity System all you had to do was buy the particular piece you needed, and you could be sure it would fit your musket.

Soon it was possible to make all kinds of complicated machinery much cheaper than ever before. Delicate machines could be made by the thousands, and without using expensive and highly trained workers. Even before the Civil War, locks and watches were cheaper in America (where they were made by the Uniformity System) than they were in countries where there were many skilled locksmiths and watchmakers.

This is what we mean by "mass production." It means producing lots of things of the same kind. It means, as Whitney explained, using the skill of the machine instead of the skill of the worker. When things were produced this way, they were much cheaper. More people could afford to buy. This in turn encouraged other people to make more cheap things to sell. The worker's time was worth a lot more. Now he could produce more of anything—guns or locks or watches—in a single day than ever before. The employer could afford to pay him more, and still make a profit.

All this changed the worker in America. In England, for example, a young man had to work for years as an apprentice before he finally became a master gunsmith. But in America a young man could work at making guns without

American factories like this one in a pleasant rural countryside startled Europeans, who were accustomed to find them in murky cities. A print by Nathaniel Currier.

even being an apprentice. He simply needed to learn how to run the machine that made one part of a gun. The American machines became more specialized. The American people were less special-ized. Here it was more important that you have general intelligence so you could handle the expensive and compli-cated machinery. Here the worker had to be quick at learning new ways.

CHAPTER 19

Do-It-Yourself Doctors

The wound of an Indian's arrow or the bite of a rattlesnake called for speedy treatment. A man had to be his own doctor.

This was all very different from the way it was in England. Over there dur-ing the colonial period anyone who could afford it would call in a learned physician. The sign of a physician was his gold-headed cane. He was a digni-fied man who commonly wore a pow-dered wig, a coat of red satin or brocade, short breeches, stockings, and buckled shoes. This "Doctor of Physick" knew Latin and Greek and had been to the university, where he had acquired lots of technical terms. But, oddly enough, he was squeamish about the human body. He would not dirty his hands,

much less let them be stained with blood. Of course he would not dress wounds or perform operations. He thought he was above all that, because he was a member of an exclusive guild. His monopoly was called the Royal College of Physicians, with headquarters in London.

Surgery—the performing of opera-tions—was the job in England of quite another man, a member of the Guild of Barber-Surgeons. Since he dirtied his hands, he was a member of a lower class. Of course he was not supposed to know learned languages, or to read books, for he was simply a craftsman who knew how to carve and cut and sew up the human body. By the eighteenth cen-tury there was still another division of jobs between the barbers (who cut hair, trimmed beards, and pulled teeth) and the surgeons, who performed all other operations.

Pharmacy, the art of mixing medicines, was practiced by people who called themselves "apothecaries." Originally they were members of the grocers' guild, but in the seventeenth century they received royal permission for a guild of their own, and then grocers were forbidden to sell drugs. The midwife (usually a woman) was experienced in delivering babies. Any of these groups would not allow nonmembers to do their kind of work. The laws punished those who tried.

The physician, of course, lorded it over all the others. By the eighteenth century the Royal College of Physicians in London had become a snobbish social club. People were admitted because they had money and came from the "best" families, but they received almost no solid instruction. Very little practical medicine was taught at Oxford or Cambridge. What was taught in the universities was mostly grand theories about how the body was supposed to operate. But neither the professors of "physick" nor their students spent much time on the details of human anatomy. Dissecting dead bodies was still considered indecent or irreligious, and had to be done in secret when it was done at all.

In early New England, trained physicians with a university degree were scarcely to be found. Most doctoring was done by ministers and schoolmasters. John Winthrop, the first Governor of Massachusetts Bay Colony, was a leading medical adviser. His son, who became Governor of Connecticut, used to give medical advice by letter. The missionary John Eliot gave the Indians medical advice at the same time he tried to convert them. The two New Englanders who pioneered in preventing smallpox by inoculation—Cotton Mather and Zabdiel Boylston—had taught themselves all the medicine they knew.

In the South, on the remote and widely dispersed plantations, even if a trained doctor could have been found, the planter could not afford to summon him for all the ailments of his slaves. For medical treatment the owner relied on himself, his wife, or his overseer. George Washington commonly prescribed for the ills of his slaves. In his own last illness it was his overseer, not a doctor, who first treated him. When Thomas Jefferson returned to Monticello from the White House one summer, he himself gave smallpox inoculations to seventy or eighty people on his plantation, and he supervised his neighbors in inoculating another hundred. The planter's wife bore much of the burden of doctoring, for she delivered babies and was often awakened in the middle of the night to look after the dangerously ill in the slave quarters.

One of the commonest books in Virginia plantation libraries was *Every Man his own Doctor; or, the Poor Planter's Physician*. First published in 1734, it was printed and sold in large numbers by Benjamin Franklin in Philadelphia. The book offered "plain and easy means for persons to cure themselves of all, or most of the distempers incident to the climate, and with very little charge, the medicines being chiefly of the growth and production of this country."

These American amateurs often did not know what they were doing. But they had one great advantage. Unlike the English professionals, they had not been trained to use drastic and painful "remedies." Those dangerous treatments were called "heroic" remedies—perhaps because they made a hero out of the unfortunate patient. They included drinks of disgusting and indigestible concoctions (made of every conceivable substance, from urine and powdered insects to lead bullets), and "bleeding" the patient (letting blood out of his veins), which was supposed to relax him and cure almost any pain. Self-trained Americans tended to be more timid. Their treatments were at least less damaging.

Jefferson, like many other American amateur doctors, believed that when you did not really understand a disease, it was better to let nature take its course. From the beginning Americans had expected a great deal from nature. Many of the advertisements which brought them here told of the invigorating New England air, of the health-giving Virginia water, or of the magical Georgia climate.

The American belief in natural remedies encouraged Americans to learn from the long experience of the Indians. It also made them adventurous and resourceful—if sometimes overly optimistic—students of nature. Unlike the European woods, the woods of America had not been combed over by generations of botanists. Observant Americans might expect to discover wonderful new healing plants.

The gum of the white poplar tree,

they said, made a balm that would quickly heal deep wounds. They learned to make a refreshing tea from the sassafras bark. When the Indians taught them to smoke tobacco, the settlers praised it as a medicine which "purgeth gross humors, openeth all the pores and passages of the body," which prevented some ailments and cured many others—including the gout, hangovers, and fatigue. They came upon the Jamestown Weed, which today is still used as a narcotic. And they made medicines from the May apple and the witch-hazel shrub. One of their most remarkable finds was the so-called "Tooth-Ache tree," whose leaves, seeds, and bark were said to be used by the people along the Southern seacoast to cure toothache.

Of course, many of these cures were imaginary. But enough were real to encourage enterprising Americans to search their woods for balms and tonics and beverages.

One source of their extravagant hopes was the belief that God had always created a remedy for every disease and an antidote for every poison. For example, it was widely believed that, since the poisonous rattlesnake was found in America, there must be a remedy here for the rattlesnake bite. Sure enough, on the very terrain where they found the snake, they also found rattlesnake root, or rattlesnake master, plants supposed to counteract the snake's poison. "The bountiful Creator discovers his marvels in proportion to our wants," rejoiced an eighteenth century American minister-naturalist. "Every country has native remedies against its natural defects."

When the nation began to have a few

The rattlesnake, unknown in Europe, attracted special interest among travelers. Here it is drawn by Mark Catesby, an English botanist-artist who visited the southern colonies in the eighteenth century. Below: The "rattlesnake root" was so called because its resemblance to the rattlesnake led people to imagine that it had a peculiar power to cure the bite of this snake.

professionally trained doctors, these men also pioneered in botany and natural history. The study of a country's diseases and the study of its plants and animals naturally went together. Dr. Alexander Garden, who had a Scottish medical degree and practiced medicine in Charleston in the later eighteenth century, probably reported more new American plants and animals than anybody else of his time. The gardenia was named after him.

Americans learned their medicine not from classroom lectures but by working as apprentices. An American doctor would keep a young man in his house for seven years doing chores—as nurse, janitor, messenger, coachman, and assistant surgeon. The apprentice read a few

Seneca
Rattle-Snake Root.

medical books but learned mostly from his master. The young man's family paid tuition to the doctor.

The Old World differences between the physician, the barber-surgeon, and the others disappeared soon enough. When the Frenchman Marquis de Chastellux traveled through the country during the American Revolution, he called all medical men here by the name of "doctor"—"because the distinction of surgeon and physician is as little known in the army of Washington as in that of Agamemnon." The American doctor therefore had a wider experience than his English counterpart. Until well into the nineteenth century, the new nation was poor in its medical schools, and American doctors were not very learned. But even Europeans noticed that somehow the Americans were remarkably successful at curing people.

American doctors, partly because they had fewer theories, were more willing to learn from experience. "More is required of us," one of them said, "in this late settled world, where new diseases often occur." In the American West, people who faced emergencies had to act quickly and do the job themselves.

For example, on a Far West trail in the summer of 1826 a man traveling in a wagon train had his arm shattered by an accidental shot as he foolishly drew his rifle, muzzle first, from his wagon. The wound began to fester and the man was dying of gangrene. His companions in the wagon train—nothing but amateur doctors—were bold enough to save his life. They dared to amputate the arm from which the infection was spreading. One of them reported:

Their only "case of instruments" consisted of a handsaw, a butcher's knife and a large iron bolt. The teeth of the saw being considered too coarse, they went to work, and soon had a set of fine teeth filed on the back.

The knife having been whetted keen, and the iron bolt laid upon the fire, they commenced the operation: and in less time than it takes to tell it, the arm was opened round to the bone, which was almost in an instant sawed off; and with the whizzing hot iron the whole stump was so effectually seared as to close the arteries completely.

Bandages were now applied, and the company proceeded on their journey as though nothing had occurred. The arm commenced healing rapidly, and in a few weeks the patient was sound and well.

Again and again, ingenious Americans made medical history. The accidents of the backwoods, and the wounds which people suffered in their wars against the Indians, in the Revolution—and later in the Civil War—all gave medical students an opportunity to see the inside of the human body, as they never might have in a university.

William Beaumont was an army doctor trained entirely by the apprentice method. On June 6, 1822, while he was stationed at remote Fort Mackinac in northern Michigan, an employee of the American Fur Company out there accidentally received a load of buckshot in his left side. Beaumont did what he could to make the wound heal, but despite everything the hole in the victim's stomach remained open. He had the inspiration to take advantage of this rare opportunity to see directly through the unhealed opening exactly what went on in a man's stomach. He took the patient under his own roof and planned his observations.

Beaumont watched how the gastric juices worked, and then saw the effects of tea, coffee, and alcohol. The result of this was Beaumont's book, *Experiments and Observations on the Gastric Juice and the Physiology of Digestion* (1833). It laid the foundation for the study of digestion and the science of nutrition. If Beaumont had been near a city, with learned specialists to tell him that his study was impossible, would he have dared as he did?

CHAPTER 20

Wagon-Towns Moving West

When an American decided to move farther west in the years after the Revolution, he seldom went by himself. Sometimes, of course, there was a lone adventurer—an explorer, a priest, or a hunter. But that was rare. To survive and cover territory, even an explorer had to go with a large group. When Meriwether Lewis and William Clark were sent by President Thomas Jefferson to the Far Northwest in 1803 to find the riverways that poured into the Pacific and to explore the newly acquired Louisiana Purchase, they organized a group that numbered altogether forty-five men.

This was an old story. From the beginning, people came here in groups. You could not cross the ocean by yourself in a canoe. To lead men great distances into unknown territory, you had to be a good organizer. On his first voyage to America in 1492, Columbus took three ships with a crew of ninety men. When Captain John Smith landed on May 24, 1607, at Jamestown, 105 others landed with him. The crowded *Mayflower* which landed at Plymouth in 1620 carried 101 passengers.

Two hundred years later, in the early nineteenth century, Americans settling across the Mississippi traveled hundreds of miles into the great West and toward the Pacific. They also moved in groups. You might start out alone or with a few friends and family from the settled States on the Atlantic Ocean. But you were not likely to reach very far into the unknown West unless you soon joined with fifty or a hundred others.

Most of the West was still unknown. A few wagon ways had been marked off by earlier explorers, and they were the only paths through the wilderness. Nobody had put up signs telling you in which direction to go or how far you were from anyplace. If you were lucky you could find your way because so many other people and animals before you had worn a trail across the land.

The most important trails started from a little town called Independence over two hundred miles west of St. Louis, and just outside where Kansas City now stands. From there the California and Oregon Trail went up across the flat plains toward what is now Nebraska and

Emigrant families with covered wagons gathered here at Independence, Missouri, to form wagon trains for the long trip west.

Wyoming, took a famous pass through the Rocky Mountains (called the South Pass), then branched off into two paths. The Oregon Trail went up toward where Portland, Oregon, is now. The other, the California Trail, went down toward where we now find San Francisco. From Independence the Santa Fe Trail led through barren desert southwestward down to Santa Fe, then still deep in Mexican territory.

The busy little town of Independence was, as one traveler said in 1844, "the general 'port of embarkation' for every part of the great 'prairie ocean.'" At Council Grove, just outside Independence, astonishing things were happening. These did not look so unusual to Americans, but would have amazed people anywhere else in the world. People from all over, who had never seen one another

before, collected there because they all wanted to go west. Just as people in Chicago, Cincinnati, Denver, and in a hundred other places were quickly coming together forming their instant cities, so these people with wagons were forming their own kind of instant towns. These were wagon-towns, towns made to move.

It was not safe to travel alone. Indians were apt to attack a small party, but if you traveled in a large group, they might be frightened off. After General Anthony Wayne defeated the Indians at the Battle of Fallen Timbers in Ohio in 1794, Indian attacks were much rarer east of the Mississippi. Then it was less dangerous for men to travel with only their families in that part of the country. But on the other side of the Mississippi, travel in large groups kept on until after the Civil War.

With enough wagons in your party, you could make a kind of fort every night. At the end of the day's travel, the wagons would be formed into a hollow square. When wagons were arranged along the outside of a square, the space inside was like a small walled town. People were protected while they cooked their meals. They could sing and dance, or hold meetings to talk about the problems of the trip. If Indians attacked, women and children could be safe in the hollow square while the men and boys shot back at the Indians from behind the wall of wagons.

Since there was no other way of building a fence, the wagons also made a corral for the horses and oxen and other animals. If there were unfriendly Indians in the neighborhood, men were stationed on guard all night. Every man and boy had to take his turn. The more men and boys there were, the more time any one could sleep between his turns.

The covered wagon used for crossing the continent was about ten feet long, eight and a half feet to the top of the canvas. It was usually drawn, not by horses, but by three pairs of oxen. Even if two oxen were lost, the four that remained could still pull the wagon. When fully loaded, it could carry a ton.

Dragging this wagon up a hill was never easy. But it was much easier if you were in a large party. Then you could do what the Brown party did in 1846 at the head of the steep Goldstream Canyon in the Sierra Nevada Mountains. The whole party helped pull the first

"The Attack on an Emigrant Train" (1856) was the vivid recollection of a young painter who had known the Indians well. Carl Wimar had been born in Germany and moved as a boy to St. Louis in 1843, when the Indians still came there frequently to trade.

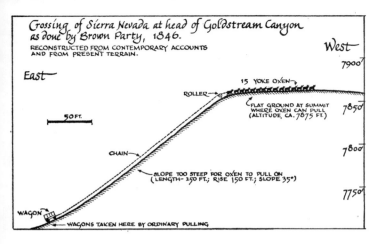

Crossing of Sierra Nevada at head of Goldstream Canyon as done by Brown Party, 1846.
RECONSTRUCTED FROM CONTEMPORARY ACCOUNTS AND FROM PRESENT TERRAIN.

East

West

7900'

15 YOKE OXEN
ROLLER
FLAT GROUND AT SUMMIT WHERE OXEN CAN PULL (ALTITUDE, CA. 7075 FT.)

7850'

50 FT.

7800'

CHAIN

SLOPE TOO STEEP FOR OXEN TO PULL ON (LENGTH = 150 FT.; RISE 150 FT.; SLOPE 35°)

7750'

WAGON

WAGONS TAKEN HERE BY ORDINARY PULLING

From The California Trail *by George R. Stewart, Copyright © 1962 by George R. Stewart. Used by permission of McGraw-Hill Book Company.*

wagon up the hill. Then fifteen pairs of oxen were attached to a chain wound around a roller (the axle of a wagon) to make a windlass. At the top of the hill oxen turned the roller on the windlass, which hoisted the other wagons, one after the other, up the hill.

Going down a steep hill was also dangerous. The brakes on the wagons were primitive. If you let your wagon coast there was always a danger of tumbling or of breaking the legs of the animals. Trees were sometimes put through the spokes of the wheels or were dragged behind to slow the wagon down. But in some places there were no trees. It was better, if you had a big enough party, to set up a windlass and ease the wagons down the hill. One high place in the North Platte Valley was actually called Windlass Hill.

When your wagon stuck in the mud, other people's oxen were yoked together to pull you out. It was dangerous driving your wagon across swift, deep streams with soft bottoms. But if you could attach your wagon to a rope hauled by wagons on the other side, you were less apt to get into trouble. At the swiftest and deepest streams, the wheels were taken off one wagon and the wagon-box became a boat. It was pulled back and forth across the river till the whole party and all their baggage were over.

The trip across the continent was long and slow. From Independence on the lower Missouri River to Sutter's Fort in California, it was about two thousand miles on the wagon trail. The normal speed for a wagon was two miles an

A wagon train fording the Platte River in 1849.

hour. At that slow speed a wagon, even without springs, might not be too bumpy on flat ground. But when the trail was especially rough, or went up or down hill, the healthy passengers preferred to walk. Even with good luck, the wagon ride from Independence to the Pacific Ocean might take five months.

The first great westward party on the Platte Route, which followed the Platte River across Nebraska and Wyoming, was led by Colonel Stephen W. Kearny in 1845. Kearny's wagon train stretched out for three miles. When so many people lived together for so long, they had to be organized. They had to make rules for health and safety. They had to appoint judges, select juries, and punish criminals. They had to keep order, arrange marriages, and perform funerals. They felt all the needs of people in Cincinnati or Chicago or Omaha, and had additional problems too. If the trip was not to take forever, they had to see that everybody kept moving. And they had to see that everybody did his share of the work and risked his share of the danger.

At Council Grove, near Independence, in the 1840's and 1850's, you could see people forming these wagon-towns. People who had never known one another were now holding meetings, passing resolutions, and drawing up regulations. They made some rules before they left Independence, and the rest after they were out on the trail.

What they did was very much like what the Pilgrims on the *Mayflower* had to do two hundred years before. They were going "through a territory where the laws of our common country, the United States, do not extend their protection." They needed a government, so they made a government for themselves. Each wagon train, with its many passengers, was a kind of *Mayflower*. Like the first pilgrims, each wagon train made its Mayflower Compact. Each had its own do-it-yourself government. They wrote out their own laws, which everybody signed.

"In view of the long and difficult journey before us," the Green and Jersey company of emigrants to California, meeting not far from Independence on

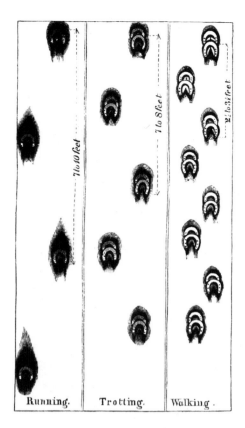

Running. Trotting. Walking.

This illustration from Marcy's Prairie Traveler *showed how to judge the speed of an Indian pony ahead.*

May 9, 1849, adopted "strict rules and regulations to govern us during our passage."

And we do . . . pledge ourselves to each other, that we will abide by all the rules and regulations that may be made by a vote of the majority of the company . . . that we will manfully assist and uphold any authorized officer in his exertions to strictly enforce all such rules and regulations. . . .

And further, in case any members of the company, by loss of oxen or mules, by breaking of wagon, robbery by the Indians, or in fact from any cause whatever beyond their control, are deprived of the ability to proceed with the company in the usual manner, we pledge ourselves never to desert them, but . . . to support and assist them to get through to Sutter's Fort, and in fact, we pledge ourselves to stand by each other . . . to the death.

Each wagon train had a captain, usually elected by a vote of the majority. Before the election there were often speeches. Since most of the people did not know one another, they could not always pick the best man. But the captain of the wagon train, like the captain of a ship, had an important job. He had to assign tasks and settle quarrels. The fate of the whole wagon train might depend on his good humor and good judgment. If the people did not like him, they could vote him out and elect someone in his place.

Many companies used a book of instructions written by Captain Randolph B. Marcy, who had battled Indians in Michigan and Wisconsin, had fought in Texas, and once commanded a hundred men on a thousand-mile march across the Rocky Mountains in winter. His book, *The Prairie Traveler, A Hand-Book for Overland Expeditions* (1859), put out by the War Department, offered lots of good advice. "First business," he said, "should be to organize . . . into a company and elect a commander. The company should be of sufficient magnitude to herd and guard animals, and for protection against Indians." He explained how to handle oxen, how to repair a wagon, and how to cross rivers. Everyone should put in some money to buy extra animals to help anyone whose animals died on the way. It was one for all and all for one!

Impatient travelers would abandon one wagon train and join another, just as people might leave Kansas City for Omaha, or Omaha for Denver, when the prospects looked better in the other place. Young James A. Pritchard and seven companions set out on April 10, 1849, from a little town in Kentucky with their mules and wagons. They took a steamer up the Mississippi to St. Louis, then went overland to Independence, where they arrived on April 22. There they spent two weeks preparing to "bid adieu to homes, friends, and happy Country." When they happened to meet a Captain Fash from Indiana, they joined his party of seventeen wagons and sixty men. But Fash's party was too slow for them. Taking four wagons from Fash's party they made up their own wagon train.

By mid-May they were deep in Indian country. But the party did not have enough wagons to make a big hollow square, and did not properly guard their animals at night. At ten o'clock on the night of May 17 a large mountain wolf began prowling around the camp. Everyone was awakened by "those hideous howls that will startle one from the profoundest sleep—and make him think that one of the fiends of the infernal regions was standing before him. And away went picket ropes and pins, at a single dash about 40 of the mules were loosed."

They decided that at last they had to organize. Three men were nominated for captain, an election was held, and Pritchard received 38 of the 40 votes. After his acceptance speech, "one universal shout rose from the crowd." They then made some laws. But Pritchard was not a successful captain. He could not keep the wagons in line. The party split again, and some of his wagons joined other parties passing on the trail.

The best organizers were the best captains of wagon trains. The Mormons were remarkably successful. With their new American religion they were looking to the west for their Promised Land. They set up instant cities of their own in Ohio and Indiana. When the Mormons prospered, their envious neighbors believed all kinds of strange stories about them, and destroyed their towns. The Mormons had to move on. In February 1846, their able leader Brigham Young began taking them across Iowa toward Utah. They built their own roads and bridges as they went. They even planted seeds along the trail so that Mormon wagon trains the next season could harvest the crops for food as they went by. One wagon train that reached Utah in October 1847 brought 1,540 Mormon emigrants in 540 wagons, together with 124 horses, 9 mules, 2213 oxen, 887 cows, 358 sheep, 24 hogs, and 716 chickens.

The Mormons were held together by their religion, which was based on *The Book of Mormon.* According to Joseph Smith, the founder of the religion, who had been raised in poverty on a farm in upstate New York, an angel Moroni had come to him in 1827 and told him where to find certain gold tablets. Then, seated behind a curtain and using magic spectacles, he deciphered the inscriptions and translated them into English. He said that the gold tablets were lost before anyone else could see them.

But the Mormons were not the only ones who expected to find a Promised Land in the unknown West. Hundreds of other wagon-towns were held together by their own vague hopes of a great future.

CHAPTER 21
Haste Makes Democracy

People who wanted to travel fast and far had to travel light. The guidebooks, like Marcy's *Prairie Traveler*, told you to take only food, clothing, tools, and weapons needed for the trip. You could not bring along your family's heavy carved furniture, or fancy hats and coats and shoes, or the elegant silverware you inherited from your grandfather. Yet all these—together with the landed estates and mansions which of course also had to be left behind—were the very things that separated the rich from the poor. Out west people made a fresh start.

Going across the desert or up and down the mountains, you might have to abandon even the few things you had brought along. James Abbey, a young man who left Indiana for California in April 1849, wrote in his diary what happened as his party crossed the desert approaching the Sierra Nevada Mountains:

August 2nd.—Started out by four o'clock this morning; at six stopped to cook our breakfast and lighten our wagons by throwing away the heavier portion of our clothing and such other articles as we can best spare. We pushed on to-day with as much speed as possible, determined, if possible, to get through the desert, but our cattle gave such evident signs of exhaustion that we were compelled to stop.
Being completely out of water, myself, Rowley, and Woodfill bought two gallons from a trader (who had brought it along on speculation), for which we paid the very reasonable price of one dollar per gallon. The desert through which we are passing is strewed with dead cattle, mules, and horses. I counted in a distance of fifteen miles 350 dead horses, 280 oxen, and 120 mules; and hundreds of others are left behind, being unable to keep up. Such is travelling through the desert. . . . A tanyard or slaughterhouse is a flower garden in comparison. . . .
Vast amounts of valuable property have been abandoned and thrown away in this desert—leather trunks, clothing, wagons, etc., to the value of at least a hundred thousand dollars, in about twenty miles. . . . The cause of so many wagons being abandoned is to endeavor to save the animals and reach the end of the journey as soon as possible by packing through; the loss of personal goods is a matter of small importance comparatively.

The American love of speed—the desire to get there first—was born in this race to and through the West. To float quickly down the Ohio, the Missouri, or the Mississippi, you put together enough rough timbers to make a crude flatboat and then let the strong current carry you. When you reached New Orleans you took the boat apart and used the lumber to build your house.

Going upstream was more difficult. By the 1820's Americans had developed a new type of steam engine to drive their boats against the current. It was called a high-pressure engine and was built less for safety than for speed. The pioneer maker of these engines was Oliver Evans, from the neighborhood of Philadelphia, who was a genius at labor-saving devices. He made a flour mill that used chutes and moving belts in place of man-power. And he actually had a plan for a steam-driven carriage that might have been a pioneer automobile. At first people said he was crazy. Then when his ideas worked they began stealing them.

The high-pressure engine was faster than anything known before. It burned lots of wood to keep up the steam, but that was not a serious objection in the virgin forests of the West. With a full head of steam the boilers in these engines sometimes exploded. But still Americans were willing to risk anything to get there first. The American motto was "Go ahead anyhow."

On these speeding Western steamboats, the accidents were appalling. Without safety valves on the crude boilers, unlimited speed meant unlimited disaster. "The democrats here never like to remain behind one another," a traveling German nobleman reported from the West about 1840. "On the contrary, each wants to get ahead of the rest. When two steamboats happen to get alongside each other, the passengers will encourage the captains to run a race. . . . The races are the causes of most of the explosions, and yet they are still constantly taking place. The life of an American is, indeed, only a constant *racing,* and why

A scene in 1849 on one of the Western trails. If emigrants had not started out traveling light, they soon learned on the trail.

Scene on the Emigrant Trail,
near Settlements, Nov. 1849.

should he fear it so much on board the steamboats?"

Captains and firemen on the Mississippi sneered at the eastern slowpokes. "It don't take no spunk to navigate them waters. . . . But I tell you stranger, it takes a man to ride one of these half alligator boats, head on a snag, high pressure, [safety] valve soldered down, 600 souls on board and in danger of going to the devil."

These Western racers, called "brag" boats, lived a short, fast life. Of all the steamboats built before mid-nineteenth century, nearly a third were lost in accidents. The main cause was explosions, which killed scores of passengers with bursts of flying wreckage, floods of steam, and scalding water. Some steamboat owners sent the passengers who had not yet paid their fares to the back part of the vessel. There, in case of explosion, they would be less likely to be killed, and the owner could still collect his fares from them.

When the railroad came, it was the same story all over again. Cautious European railroad builders, who came over here in the 1840's and fifties and sixties to see how Americans managed to lay tracks so fast over such vast distances, were horrified. Americans laid single sets of tracks, which saved time and money but of course increased the danger of collisions. Unlike European railroaders, Americans commonly did not trouble to level off hills or to lay tracks into long gentle curves or to cut tunnels. They did not bother to lay solid foundations for embankments.

All this increased the chance of speeding trains going off the rails as they tried to maneuver sharp curves, or came rocketing down steep hills. In some places hasty American railroad builders, anxious to keep working all through the winter, laid tracks right on the snow—with disastrous consequences when the spring thaws came.

American railroad builders had good reasons to hurry. State legislatures and the Congress rewarded the builders of the first railroads with big loans of money and valuable grants of land. In 1866, the self-confident leaders of the Central Pacific Railroad, which had started building from the West, actually persuaded Congress to make the laying of the transcontinental tracks into a race. The Union Pacific was building out from the East. The company that built more mileage would receive that much more money. Each company was racing against the other. They both were naturally tempted to put fast construction above everything else.

By 1850 the wrecks on the instant railroads of the West were as common as steamboat explosions had been. Experienced travelers rode in the middle cars rather than at front or back. In those days before seat belts, prudent passengers braced themselves by holding onto the seat in front of them, and they sat diagonally so they would not receive the collision shock directly on their knees. Fast American trains of the mid-nineteenth century gave you the excitement of a roller-coaster, but they were a good deal less safe.

Still the American quest for speed did have some good effects. The heavy, rigid English locomotives could not manage the sharp curves and steep in-

On hastily built American railroad bridges, accidents were common.

clines. And weak embankments and flimsy trestles sagged under their enormous weight. The famous *Stourbridge Lion*, imported from England, was the first working, steam-powered locomotive to run on American rails. It had only a short demonstration run in 1829. When it was found to be ill-suited for the American tracks, it was left on a siding to rust. A few pieces of it can be seen in the National Museum in Washington. America needed a new kind of locomotive that put less strain on the tracks and could speed around sharp curves without going off the rails.

The answer was simple enough as soon as one stopped thinking in the old European ways. English locomotives usually had only four wheels. These were big and heavy and were mounted rigidly on axles like those of the old horse carriage. They were all right on a sturdy roadbed and on a straight road. But they could not follow sharp curves. John Bloomfield Jervis, a self-taught engineer from New York, had seen the troubles with the *Stourbridge Lion*. He had very little education but lots of experience building canals and roads. He designed a new kind of railroad car. His idea, like many revolutionary innovations, was simplicity itself.

Why, Jervis asked, must we rest the whole enormous weight of the locomotive only on those four big wheels? Why must the construction be so rigid? Instead he made a separate little truck (called a "bogie") with four low wheels and put it under the front end of the locomotive. It was arranged on a swivel,

Some of the earliest American passenger cars (shown here) followed the English plan of mounting carriage bodies on a frame with railroad wheels. The large rigid front wheels of this English-style locomotive could not always hold the track in America.

---

so it could follow even a sharply curving track. Since the bogie wheels were low and small they were not so apt to derail. But Jervis still kept the big wheels under the rear end of the locomotive. Now the locomotive had more wheels. This spread the locomotive's weight over more points on the track. Then even badly built track was less likely to sink and bridges were less likely to sag.

In 1832 Jervis made a locomotive by this design, and he called it the "Experiment." This came to be called the "American-type locomotive" and has been the plan for locomotives ever since. Since you could now spread out the weight, with Jervis' plan you could make locomotives even longer and more

powerful and speedier than ever before.

People in a hurry—whether traveling by steamboat or by railroad—had to be willing to be jammed together. There was not the space to give everybody a private compartment. Any snob who was anxious to keep his proper distance from the common herd had better not go at all. On a Western steamboat the so-called "cabin" passengers included a wide range of people—from the rich and famous to those who could barely afford the extra fee to avoid being carried "deck" (or steerage) with the cattle. Among the cabin passengers, the comforts were assigned on the basis of first-come-first-served. After sleeping on the open deck or in dormitories, passen-

---

To help locomotives hold the track on the sharp curves and steep grades of American railroads, Jervis invented the "bogie truck" of low wheels which could swivel. Americans also simplified the railroad car, making it a single long box with entrances at either end.

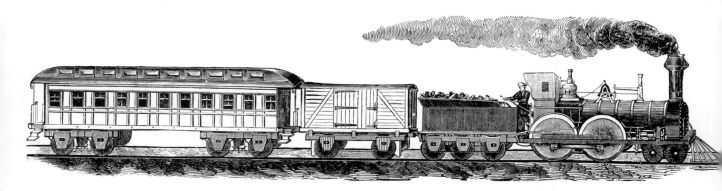

gers ate together family style at long tables. It did not matter whether you liked your fellow passengers. You still had to sleep in the same bedroom with them and eat at the same table.

The American railroad car, like the Western steamboat, was newly designed for quick construction, speed, and long distances. It also pushed people together in the new democracy of haste. The English passenger car had been made by mounting the bodies of several horse carriages on a single long frame—making a lot of separate closed compartments. The entrances, like those on the carriages, were still from the sides. You sat closely confined with six or eight other passengers who were all traveling the same "class" (first, second, or third) until the trip was over. The earliest American-type passenger cars were *one* class. Their new American design did not follow that of the old horse-carriages. Instead each American passenger car was a single, long, open, box-like compartment. You could not enter from the sides but had to enter from either end.

Like the hotel lobbies in the new cities, these spacious American passenger cars became democratic mixing places. Passengers did not sit primly in their own seats, but made themselves comfortable by removing their shoes or outer garments. They wandered about, introducing themselves, conversing, playing games, and cracking jokes. By the end of several days' journey through the vast Western spaces, they knew one another quite well.

Upper-class Europeans were embarrassed. They said Americans were always putting their noses into other peoples' business. The Viscountess Avonmore, as late as 1874, reported her annoyance at traveling with "thirty or forty human beings . . . boxed up together for seven days and nights, crammed close to each other all day, sleeping on shelves at night and in the same atmosphere."

She was shocked by the forced intimacy with so many vulgar persons. One of her fellow passengers each morning took from her pocket a set of false teeth which, she insisted on explaining, she did not sleep in because they were so expensive and she hated to use them up. The lavatory of the car could not be made private. "You cannot even tuck up your hair or roll up your sleeves," the Viscountess complained, "but some gentleman or conductor is sure to pounce upon you and remark, 'Very refreshing to get a good wash.'"

This new kind of train was perfect for the restless American. He could wander through the train, passing out the door at the end of his car and crossing the open platform into the next, where he could mingle with those passengers too. The danger of being crushed between cars or of being jolted off the train was so great that one company painted a tombstone on the doors at the ends of each car. But fidgety Americans wanted to know they were on the move. They walked on until the last car where they could admire the receding view.

When you ate in a hurry you did not have time to be upper-class or elegant. The differences between passengers with polished manners and those who had never used a napkin quickly disappeared. From time to time, the train stopped—but only for a few min-

"Ten Minutes for Refreshment," an advertisement for A&P tea and coffee. A sign by the door said: "The bell rings 2 minutes before the train starts."

utes—to feed the passengers. If you did not want to go hungry, you had better run out and grab what you could.

"The cars stop," recorded the British naval captain Frederick Marryat in 1839, "all the doors are thrown open, and out rush all the passengers like boys out of school, and crowd round the tables to solace themselves with pies, patties, cakes, hard-boiled eggs, hams, custards, and a variety of railroad luxuries too numerous to mention. The bell rings for departure, in they all hurry with their hands and mouths full, and off they go

again until the next stopping-place." The dining car did not come into use until 1863.

The "lunch counter"—in a railroad station or elsewhere, where people in a hurry could grab a bite—was an American invention of this period. Europeans complained that it was actually designed to keep a person so uncomfortable that he would eat quickly to make way for another customer. The surest way to indigestion, they said, was an American train trip!

CHAPTER 22
Political Parties for All

Newcomers were nearly everywhere after about 1820. Only the old seaboard South failed to attract them in large numbers. The cities on the Atlantic began to fill up with immigrants—especially Irish and Germans. In Kansas City, Chicago, Omaha, Denver, and in other Western cities, everybody was a newcomer. Out there you could hardly respect a man because his grandfather was rich or famous—for the simple reason that you did not know his grandfather. Every man had to stand on his own feet. And every man wanted to vote.

The old cozy rule by a few gentlemen was out. It had worked in colonial Virginia only because there were enough well-to-do families who had lived in that same colony for many years. George Washington was the great-grandson of John Washington, who had come to Virginia back in 1657. Jefferson was the great-grandson of a Thomas Jefferson who was living in Virginia in 1677.

The aristocrats of Virginia were respected partly for their ancestors. Much of their wealth and power came from relatives. They lived in mansions like Mount Vernon or Monticello, where they presided over large plantations. In the days of the Virginia Dynasty political parties had resembled clubs more than ways of grouping all Americans. And they tended to be run in private by their few aristocratic leaders.

A new American politics grew in the new cities, and in the older cities now overflowing with newcomers. Fed by every conceivable means of transportation—wagon trains, canals, transatlantic steamers, Western steamboats, and railroads—American cities multiplied and grew. When George Washington was inaugurated there were only *five* American cities of more than ten thousand people, and the largest city in the United States still had a population of less than fifty thousand. By the time of the Civil War, there were to be nearly *one hundred* American cities with a population of more than ten thousand each. By then the largest American city, New York, had over a million people. And even Philadelphia, with over half a million, was ten times the size of the biggest city in 1790.

More cities meant more politics—and a new kind of politics. People sprinkled around on farms found it hard to come together for meetings. News traveled slowly. But city people could meet at a moment's notice. They found it easy to organize, to talk with candidates, to discuss policies, to arrange debates and parades and demonstrations. Long before the Civil War it was plain that American political parties and campaigns and elections were going to be quite different from those anywhere else in the world.

Under the Constitution each State could decide for itself which of its citizens could vote. You might be a respectable farmer or an honest businessman, but you still could not vote by the laws of your State if you did not own quite enough property. Then, in the early nineteenth century, in the Age of Newcomers, one State after another changed its laws. By 1850 nearly every adult white man could vote. Most Negro Americans were still slaves, and even those who were free were rarely allowed to vote. Women would not have the vote until the Nineteenth Amendment to the Constitution in 1920.

Some of the first States to open up voting were in the West. In Ohio, for example (which in those days was still "West"), there were no "old families." The Ohio Constitution of 1802 gave the vote to almost all adult white men. And so did the constitutions in other new Western States—Indiana (1816), Illinois (1818), and Alabama (1819)—and the new Eastern State of Maine (1820).

Meanwhile, in the older States, the pressure was on to make voting more democratic. Many of the original thirteen States revised their constitutions. Connecticut (1818), Massachusetts (1821), and New York (1821) gave up the property requirement for voting. In some older States there was a bitter struggle. John Adams—who had helped write the Declaration of Independence, had been a leader in the Revolution, and was founder of a "Massachusetts Dynasty"— was chairman of the Constitutional Convention in Massachusetts in 1820. He warned of anarchy and mob rule if Massachusetts put the vote in the hands of men who had no property.

In aristocratic Virginia, change was slow. Madison, Monroe, and Chief Justice John Marshall—all members of the Virginia Dynasty—wanted to keep the property qualification. Even after the new Virginia Constitution of 1831 about one-third of the adult white men (about eighty thousand people), and all the Negroes, still were not allowed to vote. It was 1851 before Virginia abolished the property requirement. But Virginia was an exception. By 1828 about twice as many Americans could vote as could vote twenty years before.

At the same time the power to choose delegates to the Electoral College (in other words, to decide who would be President of the United States) was given to the voters themselves. By 1828, there were only two States in the Union (South Carolina and Delaware) where the delegates to the Electoral College were still chosen by the State legislature.

There was a change, too, in the way people cast their ballots. In colonial Virginia (and in some other colonies, too), a man voted by announcing his choice aloud to people standing around the village green. This way of voting, which had been brought over from England, continued in some States even after the Revolution. It was surely not the way to guarantee a poor man his right to vote for anyone he really wanted. In some States soon after the Revolution, people began writing their votes on a paper ballot. Since there were no printed ballots, the voter had to write out for himself all the names of the people he wanted to vote for. In the Pennsylvania election of 1796, for example, even if you had the right to vote, the only way you could vote for President of the United States was to write down the names of fifteen different electors on your ballot.

Someone tried printing "tickets" with

the names of his party's candidates, and then gave these to voters so they could copy the names on their ballots. In some States the government itself began printing ballots with all the candidates' names already on them. Massachusetts, for example, began this in 1830. Then all the voter had to do was put a mark beside the names of the candidates of his choice and put the ballot in a sealed box. This way of voting was much more private than the old Virginia way of announcing your choice out loud. People who were not educated enough to spell a lot of names now could vote without making mistakes.

A "party ticket" was the new name for the list of candidates supported by a political party. "Ticket-making" became a popular pastime. But who would make up the official party "ticket"? The old "caucus" where a few leaders got together and privately chose the candidates would no longer do. Everybody wanted his say—not only about who was elected, but even about who was nominated.

To do this new job of ticket-making, the parties began to hold conventions. Members of the party in each county met to choose delegates to a State Convention. There the delegates would meet

"The Verdict of the People" shows an election day in Missouri in 1854. The painter, George Caleb Bingham, had been born in Virginia but as a child had moved west to Missouri with his family. An active politician himself, he liked to paint political scenes.

to make up their party ticket. They listed their candidate for Governor and for all the other offices in the State—and they chose a candidate for President of the United States.

The State Conventions were great fun. In the days before movies or radio or television, and when other public entertainment was scarce, farmers and villagers were delighted to have an excuse to visit the big city. A State Convention was less like a solemn committee meeting than like a church picnic or a State fair. People exchanged jokes and gossip, and enjoyed plenty of refreshments. Incidentally, of course, delegates gave orations about their candidates, talked about party politics, and gave three cheers for the party. By the late 1820's and the 1830's State Party Conventions were being held all over the country.

In 1840 the Whigs pretended that their candidate was a simple man of the people.

American politics was beginning to be nearly everybody's hobby.

The next step, of course, was the National Party Convention. In the presidential election of 1832, for the first time, National Nominating Conventions were held by all the major parties that offered candidates.

The spacious new American-style hotels—"Palaces of the Public"—were convenient headquarters for candidates and for parties at their conventions. One reason why so many early National Conventions were held in Baltimore was that city-boosters there had built one of the grandest hotels in the country. Barnum's City Hotel was an elegant six-story building with two hundred apartments.

These National Party Conventions were even livelier and more festive than the smaller State Conventions. They provided a larger audience for rousing speeches by famous men. They whipped up enthusiasm for the party platform and for the party's candidates.

The colorful State Conventions and the wild celebrations at the National Conventions—all vividly reported in the newspapers—prepared people for a rip-roaring campaign.

Here was a new and very American public entertainment. It was a kind of national circus, far bigger than a county fair or a State fair. There were brass bands, barbecues, and lots of jokes and talks and stunts. Never anywhere else in the world had there been anything quite like an American national campaign.

Of course the national campaign had a serious purpose—to elect a President of the United States. When they created the office of President of the United States, the men who wrote the Constitution had, without ever intending it, paved the way for the new American party system. For the President was supposed to speak for *all* the people. Since he had to be elected every four years, this offered one regular occasion when the whole country had to worry about the same question: Who was the *man* best qualified to lead them?

On this question everybody could have an opinion. For everybody, whether or not he can read, or whether or not he is interested in politics, has an opinion about other men. As American politics became more and more democratic, as more and more people could vote, the personality of leaders became more and more important. A new type of man was put up for President.

The aristocratic members of the Virginia Dynasty—Washington, Jefferson, Madison, and Monroe—did not like to shake hands or kiss babies. Washington was a solemn man with a quick temper. He was not a good public speaker. Even his Farewell Address had not been spoken by him, but had been printed in a newspaper. Jefferson also was a poor speaker. John Adams and his son John Quincy Adams—of the Massachusetts Dynasty—were also aristocratic, dignified men who did not like crowds.

After 1828, when many more people had a voice in politics, men like these were no longer the best presidential timber. To sell a man to the American voters, he had to be popular. Or at least you had to be able to make him popular.

Andrew Jackson, who was elected in 1828, was the first of this new type of President. His father had come over from Ireland only two years before Andrew was born. Both his parents as well as his two older brothers had died before he was fifteen, and he never went to college. He was a self-made man. Settling in the fast-growing Western town of Nashville (even before Tennessee became a State), Jackson grew up with the place. He helped write the first Constitution of the State in 1796, then he represented Tennessee as Congressman and as Senator, and was a judge of the Supreme Court of the State. In 1804, with an impressive public career behind him, he "retired" to private life at the age of thirty-seven.

In the second war against Great Britain, the War of 1812, Jackson became a general. He was hailed as a hero when he defeated the British at New Orleans on January 8, 1815. This did not have any effect on the outcome of the war because two weeks before (although Jackson did not know it) a peace treaty had already been signed at Ghent in Belgium.

Jackson transformed American politics. Unlike Jefferson, who was a man of learning and who liked to speak of the international Republic of Letters, Jackson was proud of not being literary. He was not good at spelling, and once even said that he had no respect for a man who could think of only *one* way to spell a word!

Although Jackson was the first new-style President, the first campaign in the new style was the presidential election of 1840. When the Whig Party

The candidate Harrison, widely advertised as a simple backwoods farmer, actually lived in this grand mansion with a thousand acres of land. His father had been a Governor of Virginia.

held its National Nominating Convention in Harrisburg, Pennsylvania, on December 4, 1839, it passed up the able Senator Henry Clay of Kentucky because he had made too many enemies. Instead the Whigs chose a general, William Henry Harrison, although he had been nominated by them four years before and had lost. They thought he could win this time. His main qualification was that he had won a couple of battles against the Indians, and that he had very few enemies.

Since the Whigs had a reputation for being conservative and upper-crust, they had to make a special effort to appeal to the common people. For this purpose, Harrison was a good candidate. He had lived in the West a good deal, and had helped pass a law which gave land to Western farmers. The Whigs then nominated John Tyler of Virginia for Vice-President.

Against Harrison, the Democratic Party (the old party of Andrew Jackson) in their convention renominated Martin Van Buren of New York. Van Buren was a lawyer and an extremely clever politician, who had been Andrew Jackson's right-hand man. He was Vice-President under Jackson, and then served as President after defeating General Harrison in the election of 1836.

Oddly enough, the keynote of the campaign of 1840 was set by an anti-Harrison newspaper in Baltimore. What Harrison really wanted, they sneered, was not to be President at all, but simply to have a barrel of hard (alcoholic) cider to get drunk on, and a log cabin to live in. The Whigs now had their clue. They eagerly took up the cry: Hurrah for the log cabin and hard cider! Being an ordinary man who lived in a log cabin and liked to drink cider, they said, was no disgrace! On the contrary, that proved Harrison was a real man of the people.

They held a great rally in Baltimore on May 4, 1840. It opened with the firing of cannon. The Whigs boasted that 25,000 people marched in their parade and 75,000 stood by to watch. Eight log-cabin floats pulled by horses moved in the endless procession. Out of one log-

cabin chimney came smoke (supposed to show that a squirrel was roasting inside) while several supporters kept drinking hard cider from the barrel at the cabin door. "An army of banners" waved in honor of Harrison. Thousands wore campaign buttons with Whig and Harrison slogans.

The log-cabin idea had great appeal. General Harrison had really been born of an old, well-to-do Virginia family, and he lived in a mansion. But his supporters soon invented a log cabin that he was supposed to have been born in.

Instead of arguments, Whig supporters of General Harrison shouted songs and slogans. The General had supposedly won his greatest victory against the Shawnee Indians at the Battle of Tippecanoe (a small creek that ran into the Wabash River). "Tippecanoe and Tyler Too!" became their battle cry. This was the most popular song of the campaign (sung to the tune of "Little Pig's Tail"):

The new style in Presidential campaigns (Baltimore, 1840).

What has caused the great commotion, motion, motion
Our country through?
It is a ball a rolling on.
For Tippecanoe and Tyler too—Tippecanoe and Tyler too,
And with them we'll beat little Van, Van, Van,
Van is a used up man,
And with them we'll beat little Van.

Parading along while they sang this nonsense-song, men pushed huge balls—taller than a man. Sometimes a crowd would push their ball long distances, just to prove there *was* a ball "rolling on" for their hero. At the Harrison rally in Baltimore a crowd arrived with an enormous ball they had pushed with their own hands for over a hundred miles—all the way from Allegheny County in far western Maryland! Rallies all over were celebrated with tasty barbecues, washed down from free-flowing barrels of intoxicating cider.

Voters could not resist these appealing arguments. Harrison was elected, but he caught pneumonia within a month of his inauguration and died. Many people said the strain of the campaign had been too much for him.

These political high jinks looked pretty silly to people who came from countries where politics was the solemn preserve of the respectable few. Was this the curse of democracy? Or was it simply that a democratic country had to have its democratic politics? The people shared a good-natured enthusiasm for their country, for their party, and for their leaders. If they were not so solemn, they also were not so angry at their political opponents. If politics was a game, then both winners and losers were more

likely to be good sports. The future of the nation, the prosperity of workers and businessmen, and the issues of peace and war might depend on who won or lost. But good-humored politics could remind all Americans of how much they had in common.

After Jackson, candidates for President were usually "men of the people." Often they were popular because they were military heroes. After "The Hero of New Orleans" there was General Harrison ("Hero of Tippecanoe"), General Zachary Taylor ("Hero of Buena Vista"), and General Franklin Pierce, who had led volunteers in Mexico. A Presidential candidate now was supposed to be an everyday man, as common as an old shoe. He might be "Old Hickory" (Andrew Jackson), or "The Farmer of North Bend" (Harrison), or "Old Rough and Ready" (Taylor), or "The Rail-Splitter" (Lincoln). If you expected your party to win, you had better choose someone whom you could imagine being born in a log cabin.

The ideal candidate did not always make an ideal President. The problems of the nation by 1828 were deep and complicated. Although there were many ties to hold people together, the United States was really beginning to come apart at the seams. The seams were the boundaries of the States. The new issues were too deep to be wished away with songs and slogans or to be washed away in hard cider. The campaign might be jolly. But worrisome problems faced a new President when he finally reached the White House. It would take more than songs and slogans to hold the young nation together.

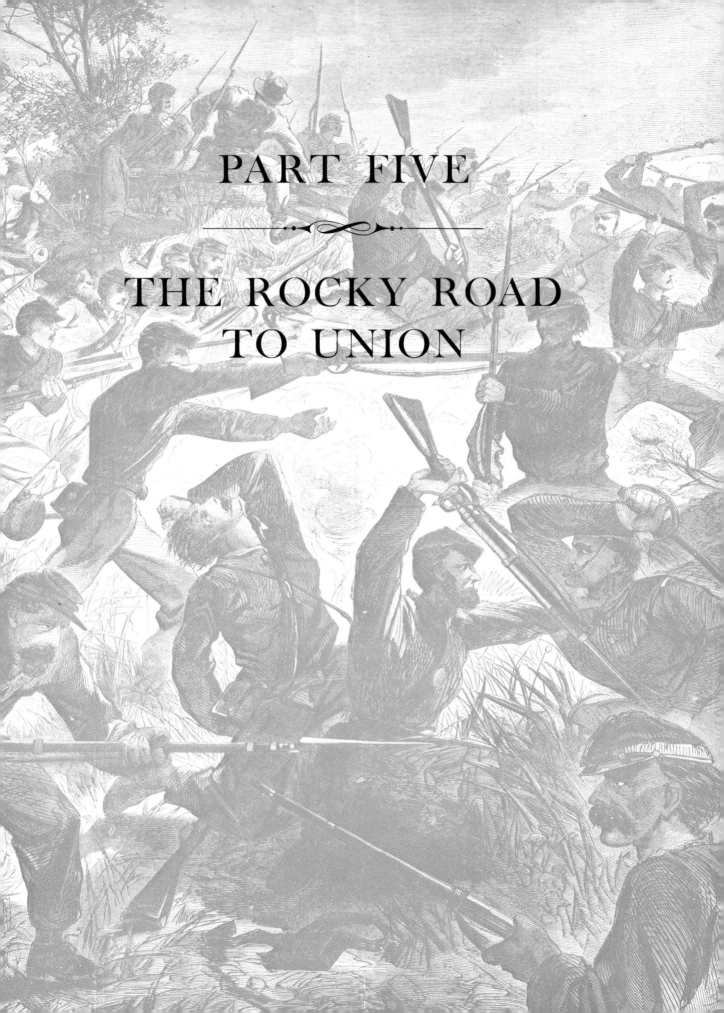

PART FIVE

THE ROCKY ROAD TO UNION

As the United States sprawled across the continent, the nation did not grow all in the same way or at the same pace. While some cities—Chicago, Omaha, Denver, and San Francisco— grew fast and prospered, others were left behind. They became ghost towns, or disappeared without a trace. The different States and different regions flourished or languished in various ways. Some people dreamed of gold and found it. Others found only rocks and disappointment. Some tried to raise crops which the soil would not nourish or where the rain did not come.

By the time of the Civil War, some regions of the United States were as different from others as, a century before, life in crowded, civilized Great Britain had been different from life in the far-off American colonies. Boston, New York, and Philadelphia already had universities and libraries and museums and a culture run by Cabots and Lawrences and Lowells and Peabodys and Livingstons and Rushes—proud "old" families. Life in the crude mining camps of Dead Man's Gulch or Virginia City was as different as possible from the ways of the elegant town houses of Charleston or New Orleans, or of the planters' mansions in Virginia.

Texas was actually a separate nation from 1836 to 1845. California, also, was briefly independent. The lonely wheat farmer or cattleman of the Great Plains of Nebraska or Iowa felt the hundreds of miles separating him from the lively crowds of Pittsburgh, Chicago, Milwaukee, or Omaha. There were many different American ways.

Could the Constitution that had been made to hold together thirteen seaboard States now bind a continent? Was it possible for a whole nation to be dedicated to the proposition that all men are created equal?

CHAPTER 23

Slavery Conquers the South

The Civil War was both the simplest and the most complicated event in American history. It was the simplest because the real issue can be summarized in one word: slavery. But it was the most complicated because, as Southerners still say, it was a "War Between the States."

The eleven seceding States, which made up the Confederate States of America, contained nine million people. On both sides there were many different kinds of people and many ways of life. In the North there were many who did not want to abolish slavery, and in the South there were many who did. In the North were many people who did not care about slavery one way or another, and in the South were many people who did not own slaves and did not make their money from slavery.

Slavery did not belong in the United States. The puzzle, then, is not why there was so much trouble over slavery. The real puzzle is how slavery became so strong, and how some white Southern Americans (even if they did not themselves own slaves) came to believe it was the very foundation of their life. If we can understand this, then we may understand why there had to be a war against slavery in order to save the Union.

In ancient times slavery was found everywhere. When one people defeated another in war, the losers, instead of being massacred, were often enslaved and made to serve the winners. In the Middle Ages, too, slavery was widespread in Europe. But beginning in the sixteenth and seventeenth centuries, out-and-out slavery was gradually displaced. Twenty years before the Pilgrim Fathers sailed, an English judge said that "England was too pure an air for slaves to breathe in."

But slavery was destined to have a new life in the New World. For many white Europeans, America meant a new freedom. For many others—especially for Negroes brought from Africa—America meant a new slavery. Under the old system of empires, as we have seen, the European mother country wanted from her colonies the things she could not produce herself. In addition to gold and silver, these were products like tobacco, rice, indigo (a plant of the pea family that made a deep blue dye), cotton, and sugar cane—crops which grew only in a warm climate.

The climate of the new colonies in South America and the Caribbean was ideally suited for these tropical crops. But these particular crops needed lots of labor. Hard work in the hot sun did not appeal to men who had left Europe for a better life. It was not easy to find workers. The Portuguese in Brazil and

Loading plan for a ship which carried slaves from Africa to America.

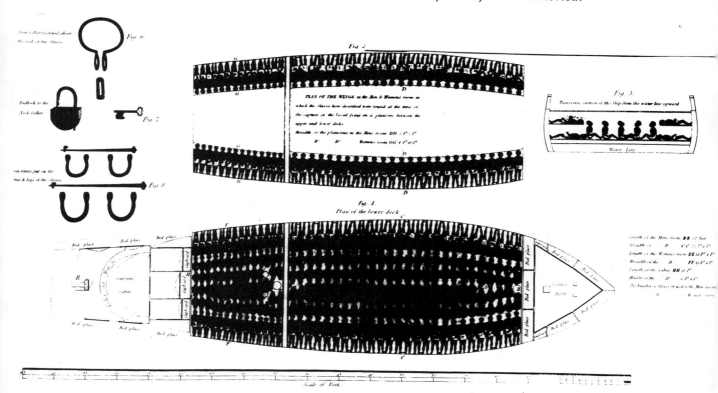

other colonists in Latin America solved their problem for a while by making slaves of the Indians. But there were not enough Indians. Harsh treatment, exhausting work, and diseases imported from Europe killed off many of them.

The Portuguese looked for other sources of labor. They began importing from Africa Negroes who had been sold into slavery by their tribal chiefs or who were captured by slave catchers. These unfortunate Negroes were stowed like livestock in ships which brought them across the Atlantic. Their misery was beyond our imagining, but since profits were high, the slave traders brought over these prisoners by the thousands. A full century before Captain John Smith landed at Jamestown in Virginia, there were parts of Brazil where there were twenty Negro slaves for every white worker.

The first Negroes, unwilling immigrants, were brought to Virginia from Africa in 1619. By the early eighteenth century Negro slaves were being imported into Virginia by the thousands. Year by year slavery was becoming more important in the life of the colony.

Thoughtful Southerners began to worry. Thomas Jefferson was especially concerned. When he made up the list of George III's crimes against mankind for the Declaration of Independence, the final item—the worst crime of all—was that the King had encouraged the slave trade. "He has waged cruel war against human nature itself, violating its most sacred rights of life and liberty in the persons of distant people who never offended him, captivating and carrying them into slavery in another hemi-

sphere, or to incur miserable death in their transportation thither." But in order not to hurt the feelings of Southern slave owners or of Northern slave traders, this item was taken out before the Continental Congress adopted the Declaration.

Jefferson continued to worry about what slavery did to the slaveholder. He explained in his *Notes on Virginia* (1783) that every slaveholder became a tyrant, and his children learned bad habits. "The parent storms, the child looks on . . . puts on the same airs in the circle of smaller slaves, gives a loose to the worst of passions, and thus [is] nursed, educated, and daily exercised in tyranny." In Virginia, Jefferson already saw "an unhappy influence on the manners of our people produced by the existence of slavery among us."

After Eli Whitney made his simple new machine in 1793 for separating the cotton fuzz from the cotton seeds, cotton became the great crop of the South. The more important cotton became, the more important was slavery. Slaves were used to plant and cultivate and pick cotton, and to work the cotton gins. Now planters aimed "to sell cotton in order to buy Negroes—to make more cotton to buy more Negroes."

Southerners soon began to say, "Cotton is King." And Cotton was a very whimsical King! For the price of cotton depended not only on the weather and the size of the crop. It also depended on how much the cotton-cloth manufacturers in Birmingham, England, or in Lowell, Massachusetts, were willing to pay. People in the South could not imagine a world without cotton. It also

RAFFLE

Mr. Joseph Jennings respectfully informs his friends and the public that, at the request of many acquaintances, he has been induced to purchase from Mr. Osborne, of Missouri, the celebrated

DARK BAY HORSE, "STAR,"

Aged five years, square trotter and warranted sound; with a new light Trotting Buggy and Harness; also, the dark, stout

MULATTO GIRL, "SARAH,"

Aged about twenty years, general house servant, valued at *nine hundred dollars*, and guaranteed, and

Will be Raffled for

At 4 o'clock P. M., February first, at the selection hotel of the subscribers. The above is as represented, and those persons who may wish to engage in the usual practice of raffling, will, I assure them, be perfectly satisfied with their destiny in this affair.

The whole is valued at its just worth, fifteen hundred dollars; fifteen hundred

CHANCES AT ONE DOLLAR EACH.

The Raffle will be conducted by gentlemen selected by the interested subscribers present. Five nights will be allowed to complete the Raffle. BOTH OF THE ABOVE DESCRIBED CAN BE SEEN AT MY STORE, No. 78 Common St., second door from Camp, at from 9 o'clock A. M. to 2 P. M. Highest throw to take the first choice; the lowest throw the remaining prize, and the fortunate winners will pay twenty dollars each for the refreshments furnished on the occasion.

N. B. No chances recognized unless paid for previous to the commencement.

JOSEPH JENNINGS.

Abolitionists argued that slavery destroyed civilization by leading men to treat their fellows as if they were mere things. This advertisement for a Southern raffle announced that the prizes were a horse and a 20-year-old slave girl.

---

became harder and harder for them to imagine a world without Negro slaves.

Every year the Negro population in the South increased. In cotton-growing regions, Negroes began to outnumber whites. For example, in Tidewater Virginia east of the Blue Ridge Mountains, in 1830 the Negroes were in the majority by 81,000. When people in the South began to think about this, it terrified them. Wise men like Jefferson and Madison were convinced that in the long run you could not have a decent life for *anybody* where anybody else was not free. The American Colonization Society, headed by ex-President Madison, aimed to rid the country of slavery by gradually exporting all Negroes to Africa.

By 1831 so many people in Virginia were worried about slavery that the new Governor, who himself owned twelve slaves, tried to persuade the State legislature to make a plan for gradually abolishing slavery. The Virginia State legislature held a Great Debate on slavery, which lasted most of the month of January 1832. They offered arguments, for and against. All sorts of suggestions were made on how to abolish slavery or how to lessen its evils. On January 25 the legislature voted: 58 for abolishing and 73 for keeping slavery. It was a narrow margin. And it was a tragic mistake. It meant that if slavery was to be abolished in Virginia, it would have to be by force from the outside.

The importing of slaves from abroad had been prohibited by Congress beginning in 1808, the earliest time allowed by the Constitution. The British had abolished the slave trade all over their empire in 1807, and then abolished slavery itself in 1834. But slave trading still flourished inside the South.

Foreign travelers who came to the United States were shocked. In the "Land of the Free" there were more slaves than in all Europe. How could a free people tolerate a tyranny which the Old World had left centuries behind?

During the generation following the American Revolution, slavery had been abolished in most Northern States. Into his draft that later became the basis of the Northwest Ordinance of 1787, Jefferson had put a law forbidding slavery northwest of the Ohio River. In 1830, of the two million Negro slaves in the United States, nearly all were in the South. There they made up more than a third of the population. Slavery, then, was mainly a Southern problem.

Why did not people in the South settle the problem for themselves? Ever since the American Revolution, some leading Southerners—like Jefferson and Madison and Chief Justice John Marshall—had seen that slavery was a dangerous evil. "I tremble for my country," warned Jefferson in 1783, "when I reflect that God is just; that his justice cannot sleep forever . . . the way [is] I hope preparing, under the auspices of heaven, for a total emancipation . . . with the consent of the masters, rather than by their extirpation."

Why didn't it happen that way, "with the consent of the masters"? There are a number of reasons. Southerners became accustomed to slavery. Most—

perhaps as many as three-quarters—of the white people of the South never themselves owned a slave, and were not even members of a slave-owning family. But nearly everybody got tangled in the web of slavery.

Free white men did not want to work alongside slaves. Hard labor came to be "slave labor." Work took on the stigma of the slave. While cities sprouted elsewhere, the South for the most part remained a land of farms and plantations. Partly because there were fewer cities, opportunities were scarcer in the South. Very few new immigrants came from abroad to settle there. Because the South lacked immigrants, it lacked new ideas. It was often immigrants who wanted to shake things up, so they could have their chance. But no one shook up the South.

CHAPTER 24

The Splitting of the Nation

We will never know whether the South would have done its own job of housecleaning, whether it would have abolished slavery on its own. For things were happening outside the South which made it hard for Southerners to keep their heads.

After the Revolution, groups in Northern cities, especially in New England, formed clubs to fight slavery. They called themselves "abolitionists." They collected lots of unpleasant facts about slavery, put them in books and pamphlets and magazines, and sent them all over the country. Of course, there were plenty of unpleasant facts to be told—

about the mistreatment of individual slaves, and the separation of Negro families.

Theodore Dwight Weld, a New England minister, started his career on a crusade against alcohol. Then, inspired by English abolitionists, he began to fight slavery. In 1839 he published *Slavery As It Is: Testimony of a Thousand Witnesses,* put together from items he had sifted from twenty thousand newspapers.

The book was a chamber of horrors. His purpose, Weld wrote, was to "see the inside of that horrible system of oppression which is enfibred with the heart strings of the South. In the advertisements for runaways we detect the cruel whippings and shootings and brandings, practiced on the helpless slaves. Heartsickening as the details are, I am thankful that God in his providence has put into our hands these weapons [these facts] prepared by the South herself, to destroy the fell monster."

Nearly everybody likes to read horror stories. The book sold for only 37½¢ a copy and nearly everybody could afford one. There was a bargain price of $25.00 per hundred for people who wanted copies to give away. The book spread all over the North. Within the first four months it sold 22,000 copies, within a year more than 100,000. Northerners now began to get their picture of the South from Weld's book and from others like it. When Charles Dickens, the English novelist, wrote his book about America he copied his stories about the South from *Slavery As It Is*.

In Weld's book Harriet Beecher Stowe found much of the ammunition for her own anti-slavery novel. While she was writing *Uncle Tom's Cabin*, she said, she used to sleep with Weld's book under her pillow. *Uncle Tom's Cabin* came out in March 1852. In the story the Christ-like Negro, Uncle Tom, finally is flogged to death by the brutal slave dealer, Simon Legree, because he won't give away the hiding place of two escaped slaves.

The book quickly sold more than 100,-000 sets of an expensive two-volume edition. When it too was put out in a single cheap volume for 37½¢, within a year it sold more than 300,000 copies. It was made into plays and musical comedies.

Uncle Tom side shows at fairs and circuses played up the scene of "Eliza Crossing the Ice" with her baby in her arms, and had Little Eva yanked up to heaven by pulleys. "Uncle Tom's Cabin played here last night," said one newspaper. "The bloodhounds were good." The book sold enormously in England. It was quickly translated into French, Italian, Dutch, Swedish, Danish, Flemish, Polish, and Magyar. In the German language alone there were more than forty different translations. *Uncle Tom's Cabin* became America's all-time, worldwide best seller.

Mrs. Stowe gave one of the first copies to her Congressman one day as he was about to board the train for Washington. He started reading the book on the train. The story was so sad that he began to cry. He attracted the attention of the other passengers as he wiped the tears from his face and blew his nose. To avoid embarrassment, he got off the train at the next stop, where he rented a hotel room and sat up all night finishing the book. There, in the privacy of his room, he could weep to his heart's content. Many other people, too, reported that the book had upset them, and there must have been thousands of tear-stained copies of *Uncle Tom's Cabin*.

It is possible that, without this book, Lincoln could never have been elected President. During the Civil War, Mrs. Stowe went to see President Lincoln. "Is this the little woman," Lincoln asked her, "whose book made such a great war?"

Many abolitionists were devout Christians. They believed that Jesus hated slavery. "Do unto others as you would have others do unto you." You do not want to be a slave yourself. What right, then, do you have to enslave others? Christianity, they said, was the religion of love—love for all your fellow men. The abolitionists wanted to preach love. But before very long they were also preaching hate.

It was easy enough to go from hating slavery to hating slaveholders. And easy enough, too, to go from hating slaveholding Southerners to hating all Southerners. Since abolitionists were more interested in horror stories than in statistics, they did not advertise the fact that most white Southerners were not slaveholders. In their hatred of slavery they painted a picture of the South that had no bright spot in it. If there was any virtue in the South, why had not Southerners already abolished this monstrous evil for themselves?

Beginning in the 1830's a rising flood of abolitionist literature covered the country. It awakened Northerners to the evils of slavery. It made them hate slavery. It made them hate slaveholders. It also made them lump together all people in the South as if all Southerners wanted slavery. More and more people in the North began to hate the South and to hate Southerners.

As Northern propagandists became more and more violent, more and more unreasonable, Southerners too became more and more unreasonable. As Northerners began to attack things about the South that were not really evil, Southerners replied by defending things about the South that were not really good. Instead of worrying over how to get rid of slavery, more Southerners began to worry over how to defend slavery, and the South and themselves, against outside attack. They stopped apologizing for slavery. They stopped saying that slavery was only a "necessary evil."

Leaders in the South began to change their tune. "Slavery is not an evil," declared the Governor of South Carolina in 1829. "On the contrary, it is a national benefit." A professor at the College of William and Mary wrote an influential book putting together the best arguments in favor of slavery.

One of the strongest supporters of slavery was Senator John C. Calhoun of South Carolina. He had been Secretary of War under Monroe, then was Vice-President of the United States, and was now the leading Southern thinker. "Many in the South," he said, "once believed that it [slavery] was a moral and political evil; that folly and delusion are gone; we see it now in its true light, and regard it as the most safe and stable basis for free institutions in the world."

Calhoun was supported by many others when he called slavery a "positive good." Southern ministers said the Bible required that the Negroes be slaves. Southern "scientists" said the Negroes were an inferior race—the product of a "separate creation" that God made in the beginning on the African continent. Southern historians said that the glories of Ancient Greece were possible only because the Greeks had lots of slaves. Astonishing nonsense was written by otherwise sane people—all to show that slavery was the greatest thing that had ever happened to the human race.

The most brilliant and most extreme of these defenders of slavery was a

Virginia lawyer, George Fitzhugh. Having traveled through the North, where he saw some miserable factory workers, Fitzhugh returned South a convinced pro-slavery man.

In his curious book, *Cannibals All!, or Slaves without Masters* (1857), he went even further than those who only said that slavery was a "positive good." According to him any "free" society—that is, any society without slaves—was evil, precisely because it did *not* have slaves. Factory owners in the North were "Cannibals All." That is, they ate up the lives of poor workers, who labored long years and then were thrown away when old or sick. For all practical purposes, according to Fitzhugh, Northern workers too were slaves, but they were "slaves without masters." Nobody was required to look after them, to see they were fed and clothed.

Slaves in the South, Fitzhugh said, were more lucky. They were slaves *with* masters. They had the best kind of social security. Whatever happened, it was not their worry. They did not have to pay any bills. They had no problem of unemployment. Slavery, as Fitzhugh described it, was a kind of socialism, where all property was put in the hands of the people (the white people) best qualified to use it, for the benefit of everybody, whites and Negroes. Three cheers for slavery!

Southerners now showed they were

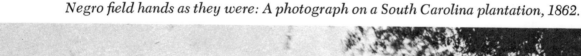

Negro field hands as they were: A photograph on a South Carolina plantation, 1862.

just as clever as the Northerners in the great national competition in name-calling. When Northerners called all Southerners torturers and monsters in human form, Southerners answered by calling all Northerners cheating, stingy, money-grubbing Yankees. A Yankee, they said, was a man without a heart—or rather his heart was in his pocketbook. He understood nothing but money.

A pamphlet that circulated in the South after 1832 told about a Yankee who was sent to Hell. Before letting the Yankee in, the Devil put him on trial, and accused him of the following crimes: (1) cheating people by selling 497,368 wooden nutmegs, 281,532 cigars made of oak leaves, and 647 wooden clocks with no works in them, (2) stealing an old grindstone, smearing it over with butter, and then selling it as cheese, (3) selling to a pious old lady a worn pair of shoes represented to be the shoes of Saint Paul. The Yankee replied that in New England where he came from these were considered "the cutest tricks." They had delighted his father, who said they proved his son a genius. Even the Devil was disgusted! And he said that Yankees were a bigger nuisance than all the rest of the world put together.

Of course, both Northerners and Southerners were wrong when they said the people in the other region were evil. But they were right when they said that the United States was being separated

---

Negro slaves in the idealized view of an unidentified pro-slavery artist.

into two different nations.

There were really many Souths. There was the "Old South," including six States (Delaware, Maryland, Virginia, North Carolina, South Carolina, and Georgia) of the original thirteen. And then there was a newer South of nine other States where slavery was also permitted. Among these Florida, which for centuries had belonged to Spain and was finally admitted as a State in 1845, was a peculiar place. It had lots of jungles and everglades, where Indian tribes still roamed. The other new Southern States —Kentucky (admitted 1792), Tennessee (1796), Louisiana (1812), Mississippi (1817), Alabama (1819), Missouri (1821), Arkansas (1836), and Texas (1845)— were as much West as South. Situated on the western side of the Appalachian Mountains, they looked away from the Atlantic Ocean. Their superhighway was the Mississippi River. They were the goal of many new settlers, and they had much of the Western spirit.

The dignified old families of Virginia and the Carolinas looked down their noses at the crude backwoodsmen of Kentucky, Tennessee, and Alabama. In the Old South, gentlemen settled their quarrels in well-mannered duels arranged by seconds and held according to elaborate old rules, under the traditional Dueling Oaks. In the newer South, life was rough. Quarrels there were more likely to be settled by a free-for-all with the Bowie knife.

One thing drew all these States together. It was not so much that they were Southern States, but that they were *Slave* States. As Southerners began to boast of slavery, slavery began to dom-

inate everything. To avoid the word "slavery," which freedom-loving men everywhere hated, Southerners began to call it their "Peculiar Institution." The Peculiar Institution was really making the South into a peculiar place.

To keep out abolitionist books and magazines, Southern States began stopping the United States mails. If a professor was suspected of not supporting slavery enthusiastically enough, he was fired. To prevent slave uprisings, Southerners wanted to arm every white man. Military academies flourished, but other kinds of schools and colleges and universities did not. Southerners began to be afraid of their own shadows. If you did not proclaim the virtues of slavery, you were probably an enemy or a traitor.

Southerners began to think they were a separate nation—which would stand or fall with slavery. Anyone who attacked slavery, they said, was attacking all the Southern people. Southerners became angrier and more passionate. Hate was brewing on all sides. Southerners began to shout: "Death to Abolitionists!"

Elijah Parish Lovejoy was a New Englander who studied to be a Presbyterian minister at Princeton, and then in 1833 settled in St. Louis, Missouri, where he began publishing a religious newspaper. Lovejoy was a fanatic. He was against lots of things—including alcoholic drinks, the Catholic Church, and slavery. He wrote strong words in his newspaper, which he sent down the Mississippi from St. Louis, Missouri, to serve the cause of abolition. But Missouri itself was a Slave State. In order to find a safer place for his newspaper, in 1836 he moved twenty-five miles up the river to Alton, Illinois, where slavery was not allowed. But the pro-slavery forces even reached up over the border. Lovejoy was in for serious trouble.

One Sunday morning his press, which had been brought up the river from St. Louis, arrived on the dock in Alton. Lovejoy was so religious that he would not do any work on Sunday, and he left the press unguarded on the river bank. That Sunday night somebody dumped it in the river. The decent citizens of Alton gave their own money to replace the press. But pro-slavery mobs destroyed Lovejoy's press again—and again.

Finally, on November 7, 1837, word spread that the Ohio Anti-Slavery Society had sent Lovejoy another press which had just arrived. Sixty young abolitionists from nearby towns gathered to defend the press. Merchants, expecting trouble, closed their stores and begged Lovejoy to leave town. He refused, saying he preferred to be a martyr. That night there was a battle at the warehouse where Lovejoy's new press was stored. An armed mob of pro-slavery men gathered, but the abolitionists' guard held them back. Then the pro-slavery forces began to set the warehouse on fire. When Lovejoy leaped out to prevent them, he was shot dead.

For abolitionists everywhere, Elijah Parish Lovejoy became a martyr. Pro-slavery men said he merely got what was coming to him.

Both sides were collecting their heroes and martyrs. It was becoming harder and harder to imagine that the peoples of the North and the South could be kept within a single nation.

CHAPTER 25

A National Tug-of-War

The powers of the national government were increasing. And the Slave States feared that those powers might be used to destroy slavery. The very same Northwest Ordinance of 1787 which had set up the Add-a-State Plan also had prohibited slavery in all the new States that would be carved from the territory northwest of the Ohio River.

When the Louisiana Purchase in 1803 added lands as large as the whole area of the original thirteen States, nervous Southern slave owners had more reason than ever to be fearful. What would happen when *those* lands were sliced up into new States? Would those States, too, be set up under some law that forbade slavery? If that should happen, then the Slave States which had once dominated the Union would become only a small minority. Then surely the new-style national government in Washington would no longer understand the South and its problems. Perhaps it would even launch a crusade against slavery and destroy the Peculiar Institution inside the original Southern States.

The only way to avoid this danger, Southern statesmen believed, was to be sure that the new States carved out of the West were equally balanced between Free and Slave. Then it would not matter so much how unevenly the population grew or how many more new Northern Congressmen might come into the House of Representatives. In the Senate, where each State had its two votes—no more and no less—Slave States still would be able to block any threatening laws. In this way the South could actually use the Add-a-State Plan to preserve slavery.

The story of how new States were added in the early nineteenth century reads like a tug-of-war. Each side added one whenever the opposite side added one. By the end of 1819, there were twenty-two states in the Union, and the sides were precisely even—eleven Slave States against eleven Free States. The population of the whole country had grown to nearly ten million. Since the North was growing faster than the South, there were about a half-million more people in the North. This meant that in the House of Representatives the North had 105 members against only 81 for the South. But in the Senate, of course, the two sides were still even.

When the Territory of Missouri applied to Congress for Statehood in 1819, the South held its breath and prepared for its first great struggle to defend slavery. Louisiana, admitted as a State in 1812, had been the first one carved out of the Louisiana Purchase. But Louisiana, where slavery had long existed, was plainly Southern. There was no question about its being a Slave State. Missouri, now, was quite another matter. For Missouri was located squarely in the middle, halfway between the north-ern and the southern boundaries of the newly purchased West. Was Missouri to be Slave or Free?

In Congress, then, the battle lines were drawn. Some Southerners already believed they were in a life-and-death struggle. If they let Missouri go Free, the Union would surely be flooded by still more and more Free States. Then it was only a question of time until the national government would abolish slavery everywhere. A new bitterness entered the halls of Congress. Northern Congressmen argued that to allow slavery into the West would be a national disgrace. As the debate went on, it simply confirmed the fears of Southerners that the Free States were out to destroy slavery, and with it the South.

The "Missouri Compromise," which Congress passed in 1820 after a whole year of debate, was not so much a compromise as a stalemate. Following the rules of the North-South tug-of-war which had already been going on for at least twenty years, each side added one State to its team. Missouri was admitted as a Slave State, while, to balance it, Maine was admitted as a Free State. At the same time the law drew a line through all the rest of the lands of the Louisiana Purchase (at 36° 30′, extending the southern boundary of Missouri) and declared that slavery would be *excluded* north of that line.

Although people at the time called it a compromise, it was not really like the compromises made by the framers of the Constitution in 1787. Those earlier compromises—for example, the one between the large and small States—were designed to give each side on every question part of what it wanted, so that everybody could consider that question settled and move on to other things. But slavery was a different kind of question. For both sides it was all-or-nothing. Both sides were simply biding their time.

Far-sighted men saw that the Missouri Compromise was nothing more than a truce which announced the opening of a fight to the finish. The aged Thomas Jefferson, retired at Monticello on his Virginia mountaintop, was saddened. It was, he said, "a fire-bell in the night . . . the [death] knell of the Union." John Quincy Adams saw it as "a title-page to a great tragic volume."

If the nation had not been growing and moving west so fast, the truce between North and South might have lasted longer. The next crisis came over Texas. Stephen Austin started an American settlement out there in the year after the Missouri Compromise. He was so successful that he soon attracted thousands of immigrants from the United States to settle in this Mexican territory. Austin was a versatile young man who had been born in Virginia, had attended Transylvania College in Lexington, Kentucky, and had lived in Missouri, Arkansas, and Louisiana. He had run a store, had directed a bank, edited a newspaper, and officered the militia, and he was a good-natured dictator.

The House of Representatives in 1822, as painted by the versatile Samuel F. B. Morse (who besides being a notable artist also invented the telegraph and the Morse Code). Here were heard some of the bitterest debates over slavery.

In 1847, before the Gold Rush, San Francisco was a mere village.

But he was a pro-slavery man, and he protected slavery in Texas.

Then in 1836, after their valiant defense of the Alamo and a victory at San Jacinto where they captured the Mexican general, the people of Texas declared their independence from Mexico. Now that Texas, on the very border of the United States, was an independent country settled and run by people from the United States, it was only a question of time until its people asked to join the Union. Texas was so big that there was no telling how many new States might be carved from her territory. And all Texas was slave country. It is not surprising, then, that when the people of Texas asked to become part of the United States and the proposal came up in Congress, Northerners again and

again voted it down. Texas, they said, was nothing but a slave-owners' clever plot to smuggle a lot of new Slave States into the Union.

For years the Northern States managed to keep Texas out of the Union. Texas was drawing the country's energy away from all other questions. At the time of the presidential election of 1844, the Texas question was more alive than ever. The popular desire for compromise was so great that the Democratic Party actually refused to nominate their best-known leader, Martin Van Buren, who had already been President once. For Van Buren had said he was against annexing Texas.

Instead, for the first time in American history, a party nominated a "dark horse," a man who was not nationally known and whom few had imagined as a candidate. He was James K. Polk, once governor of Tennessee, and a loyal Democrat. The Whigs, running the famous Henry Clay as their candidate, ridiculed the Democratic choice of a man who was unknown. It happened that earlier that year the polka had become the most popular dance in Washington. "The *Polk*-a dance," they said, "will now be the order of the day. It means two steps *backward* for one in advance."

But the Whigs were wrong, and Polk carried the day. Polk had a formula for compromise. His word was: *Expansion!* To annex Texas all by itself seemed a menace—at least to the North. But if at the same time you annexed the vast Oregon Territory, which stretched far up into the Northwest, you had something to give the North in return. That was Polk's platform. Expand everywhere at once, and then there would be something for everybody. Anyway, the very thought of stretching the nation all the way to the Pacific was exhilarating. Perhaps the nation could be united simply by marching westward together. In a divided nation, growth itself could be a kind of compromise.

And so it happened. In 1845, Texas finally was admitted as a State of the Union. The law also provided that, with the consent of Texas, not more than four additional States might some time be carved from her territory, and that the Missouri Compromise line would extend north over Texas. That was something for the South. Later that year, living up to his campaign promise, Polk claimed for the United States the whole vast Oregon Territory, which we had been sharing with Great Britain. That was something for the North.

Polk at first demanded a stretch which reached all the way up to the borders of Alaska (then owned by Russia), but he finally settled on the forty-ninth parallel, which simply extended to the Pacific the northern boundary of the rest of the nation. Now both North and South had gained large territories. New States out there would eventually add to the strength of both sides.

But for those who wanted to cement the nation and to quiet the conflict between North and South, Polk's program actually created some new problems. Mexico considered the annexation of Texas (which she said was still a part of Mexico) to be an act of war by the United States, and anyway she disputed the boundary of Texas.

Meanwhile, a new trouble spot had developed in California (still part of Mexico), where settlers from the United States were beginning to move in. The Mexican government wanted to keep all Americans out of California, for fear that it would go the way of Texas. Mexico threatened war. But Northerners feared that victory over Mexico might secure still more territory to make new Slave States in the Southwest. Over Northern opposition, Polk led us into war against Mexico.

Northern fears proved to be well founded. In 1848, after United States forces had captured Mexico City (as was expected), the helpless Mexican government gave up all claims to Texas and agreed that Texas belonged to the United States. And that was only a beginning. Before the war, Mexico had owned all the land in the Far West that reached up to Oregon from the present Mexican border, and all the lands between the Pacific Ocean and Texas. The defeated Mexico now handed all that vast tract over to the victorious United States. That included the present California and New Mexico, and most of the present States of Utah, Nevada, Arizona, and Colorado.

These lands (including Texas) were larger than the whole Louisiana Purchase or all the original United States when the Constitution was adopted. This should have satisfied any American's yen for expansion. Yet when President Polk asked the Senate to approve the Mexican treaty that gave the United States all this, a dozen Senators voted against it because they wanted to annex the *whole* of Mexico! But the treaty passed.

It took no prophet to predict that more Western lands spelled more trouble. Every new acre was a new subject for a debate—or rather, for a quarrel. Southerners did not bother to study whether these new lands were really places where slavery and the plantation system would flourish. They were thinking only about spreading the Slave Power.

In the bitterly divided nation, every stroke of national good luck became a new cause of discontent. Each section was afraid the other would somehow gain more.

By an astonishing coincidence, gold was discovered in California in the very same year when Mexico handed over

The discovery of gold in northern California in 1848 drew settlers by the thousands, so that California was ready for Statehood two years later. This print shows San Francisco in 1851.

California to the United States. Gold-rushers flocked to California by the tens of thousands. These people, too, would soon want to come into the Union as a State. But in 1849 there were thirty States altogether, and the national score-card showed fifteen Slave States against fifteen Free States. To admit the State of California, as its people requested in 1850, would break the tie.

How long could the national balancing act go on? The United States was now stretched from ocean to ocean. The boundaries on the north and the south with Canada and Mexico were now substantially settled. The slavery issue could no longer be indefinitely postponed by promising outside neighboring territory to the North or to the South. Now the conflict had to take place *inside* the established boundaries of the nation.

Early in 1850, when the Senate met to decide the future of the territories taken from Mexico, the air was more than ever charged with fear and hate. Senator Calhoun from South Carolina made impossible demands. He actually had prepared a fantastic constitutional amendment providing for the election of two Presidents—one from the Slave States and one from the Free States. Senator Seward of New York called all compromise "essentially vicious," and refused even to appeal to the Constitution. He preferred a "higher law."

Leading the forces of conciliation was the energetic Senator Henry Clay of Kentucky, who had a plan. By nature a compromiser, he had the half-hearted support of lots of people, and the enthusiasm of very few. The bundle of laws which later became the "Compromise" of 1850 was sponsored by this man whom the nation had already three times defeated for its President. He offered something for everybody, but he left the main question unanswered. California was to be admitted as a Free State (something for the North). A strong Fugitive Slave Act would protect the right of Southern slaveowners to recapture slaves who had escaped to the North (something for the South). The slave trade was abolished in the District of Columbia, where the city of Washington was located (something for the North). But slavery was still protected there (something for the South).

The biggest question—whether all the rest of the vast new areas taken from Mexico would be Free or Slave—was left unsettled. Clay's compromise postponed the answer. He provided that the people of those States should in the future decide that for themselves when they applied to join the Union. This scheme was called "popular sovereignty" by those who admired it, and "squatter sovereignty" by those who did not. It held the seeds of civil war.

Short-sighted optimists called this a "final" settlement. But a second look showed that it only put off the evil day. As usual in the years before a war, each side accused the other of acts of aggression.

Both sides were right. Both freedom and slavery *were* aggressive. The champions of each rightly believed that each must expand or die. Pro-slavery forces in the South would not leave well enough alone. They had lost California, but that simply stirred them to push harder on

"Border Ruffians" was the name given to pro-slavery men like these who invaded Kansas from Missouri in order to vote illegally or to terrorize the anti-slavery settlers.

the next round.

The next round came sooner than most people expected—in 1854. People had been moving into the lands left over from the Louisiana Purchase. It was time for them to become Territories, and to provide for their eventually becoming States. Would they be Free or Slave? Senator Stephen A. Douglas of Illinois took the lead. He argued that it was best for Congress to refuse to answer the most difficult question. He argued that the idea of "popular sovereignty" should extend even into those northern regions. Let slavery be decided "democratically" —by the people who actually lived there at the time they applied to become States.

Douglas, who was a clever politician, actually managed to get his Kansas-Nebraska Bill passed in 1854, after months of debate. It *seemed* to keep an even balance between Slave and Free by allowing future new States to decide for themselves. Actually it was a great victory for the South. For the whole Kansas-Nebraska Territory was north of the old freedom-line drawn in the Missouri Compromise back in 1820. "Popular sovereignty" now opened those lands to slavery.

If Senator Douglas thought his plan

could somehow settle the slavery issue and hold the Union together, he was soon proved wrong. His Kansas-Nebraska Act aroused a strong new political force, organized in that same year of 1854. It was called the Republican Party. And it drew together people who opposed allowing slavery into the new West.

Senator Douglas had simply marked off a new battleground. This was no longer a battleground of mere words. New Englanders formed Emigrant Aid Societies and collected money to send large numbers of anti-slavery people into

Kansas to keep it a Free State. Southerners sent in their pro-slavery settlers. "Popular sovereignty" became an invitation to civil war. Kansas soon had two rival governments, one anti-slavery and the other pro-slavery.

By mid-1856, American citizens in Kansas were killing one another over slavery. On May 21, pro-slavery forces, led by the Southern Colonel Jefferson Buford and his Kickapoo Rangers, captured, sacked, and burned the anti-slavery town of Lawrence, Kansas. Then John Brown, who believed he had been sent by God to destroy slavery and slave

A constitutional convention in Kansas Territory in 1855. The temper of the times is symbolized by the rifles close at hand.

owners, took revenge with his four sons and other anti-slavery men. In another Kansas town, Brown's party executed five pro-slavery men in the Massacre of Pottawatomie. Now less than ever could the Congress of the United States escape the great issue.

When the question came up of admitting Kansas as a State, there was not *one* Kansas government but *two!* Each claimed to be the true and only government of Kansas. Kansas would not finally be admitted as a Free State until 1861 when the whole nation was preparing for war. Back in 1856 no one was sure whether it would be Free or Slave. But everyone called it "Bleeding Kansas."

The spirit of violence reached into the very halls of the Senate. While the Kansas issue was debated, Senator Charles Sumner of Massachusetts attacked the South and several of its Senators with every insulting word he could command. Representative Preston S. Brooks of South Carolina (the nephew of a Senator from that State who had been insulted) avenged the honor of the South—not with words, but with a cane. On May 22, 1856, Brooks came up to Senator Sumner while he was seated in the Senate Chamber and beat him senseless. Brooks was reelected by his constituency, and became a Southern hero. Senator Sumner never regained his health. He became a Northern martyr, and for several years his empty seat in the Senate was a vivid symbol that many Northern and Southern leaders were no longer on speaking terms.

We can easily be misled if we think that the years from 1820 to 1860 were years of compromise. The Missouri Compromise (1820), the Compromise of 1850, and the Kansas-Nebraska Act (1854)—none of these was truly a compromise. Each was a truce in a war to the death. The issue was not to be settled by words and votes. The fate of slavery would be settled on the battlefield.

CHAPTER 26

The First Shot Is Fired

As late as 1860, some people thought the nation might avoid a civil war. Even if Americans could not agree on the issues, maybe they still could agree on a man. Maybe an American President—one man elected by all the people and speaking for all the people—could save the day. Maybe the right man could hold the Union together.

Until then the political parties had, on the whole, been *national*. The old Federalist Party of George Washington and the Republican Party of Thomas Jefferson had both drawn supporters from all parts of the country. The new Democratic Party which had elected Presidents Jackson and Van Buren and Polk, and the Whig Party which had elected Presidents William Henry Harrison and John Tyler and Zachary Taylor—both these parties, too, gathered votes from North, South, East, and West.

When the Presidential election year of 1860 approached, the Democratic Party was still a national party. The tug-of-war was going on *inside* the party, but the Democrats still had support all over the country. If the political battles could only be fought out *inside* the parties! Then the compromises would be made at the Party Conventions. And then perhaps the politicians from the North and the South could be held together (as politicians often are) simply by hope for the rewards of a political victory. Maybe the game of politics, which Americans had learned to play so good-naturedly, might take the place of the bloody game of war.

When the political parties met in their National Conventions during the spring and summer of 1860, it quickly appeared that politics was not the road to reunion. As soon as the Democratic Party opened its regular convention at Charleston, South Carolina, Southerners demanded that the party should favor protecting slavery in the territories. When Northerners voted them down at this point, delegates from eight Southern States left the convention. Even then, and after fifty-seven ballots, the convention still could not agree on a candidate for President. The convention broke up, and after

A cadet dance at West Point in September 1859. A year and a half later these young officers would be facing their classmates across the trenches.

FREE SPEECH,
FREE HOMES,
FREE TERRITORY.

PROTECTION TO AMERICAN INDUSTRY

FOR PRESIDENT
ABRAHAM LINCOLN
OF ILLINOIS

FOR VICE PRESIDENT
HANNIBAL HAMLIN
OF MAINE

A handsome, clean-cut Lincoln with his running mate, Hamlin of Maine. Lincoln did not grow his familiar beard until after his election as President. He said it was to please a certain little girl, but it may have been to give him the feel and the look of mature wisdom.

a month it met again (without the delegates of the eight Southern States). Then yet another group of Southerners withdrew. What was still left of the Democratic Party, of course, was not a national party at all. It nominated Senator Stephen A. Douglas of Illinois.

The Southern Democratic seceders gathered at Richmond, Virginia. There they named their own candidate, John C. Breckenridge of Kentucky, who was then Vice-President of the United States. He believed in protecting slavery, and he thought States had a right to secede. The damage was done! Even "national" political parties were no longer national.

The other main party in the election

of 1860 was only six years old. The Republican Party had been founded for the very purpose of opposing the spread of slavery. It was the anti-slavery party of the West and the North. Still vainly hoping for some national appeal, the new Republicans named one of the most conservative men they could find in their party. He had not made any radical statements, and he sounded like the soul of easygoing common sense. His nickname was "The Rail-Splitter" and his name was Abraham Lincoln, of Illinois.

It was a stroke of rare good luck that Lincoln happened to be there at that moment. There had never been a better symbol of all America. Lincoln's own life was a capsule history of the whole nation. His restless family had come from England to New England and then to Pennsylvania. Lincoln's great-grandfather had lived in Virginia, where he had five sons. Four of these moved on to Kentucky, Tennessee, and Ohio. In 1782, Lincoln's own grandfather had gone west to Kentucky where, four years later, he was killed by Indians while clearing his farmland in the forest. There Abraham's father was raised and there the future President was born in 1809.

Unlike other "log-cabin" candidates before him, Lincoln really was born in a log cabin. When he was only seven his family moved again—on to Indiana. And when he was twenty-one he moved with them once more, still farther west, to Illinois. Working his way up in the world, he did a little of everything. He built a flatboat and navigated it down the Mississippi to New Orleans. He did a little surveying, managed a mill, ran a country store, served as a village postmaster, and was elected captain of the militia that chased Chief Black Hawk and his Indians back into the Wisconsin wilderness.

Lincoln educated himself, and made himself into a lawyer who was especially successful before juries. But his political career had been brief and not impressive. After serving in the Illinois legislature he had one term in Congress, where he opposed the Mexican War. Then he was defeated for the United States Senate by the much better-known Stephen A. Douglas.

Lincoln had a magic in his speech. With his slow backwoods drawl, using the simple words of the Bible, he uttered the wisdom of a cracker-barrel philosopher. He sometimes told slightly vulgar jokes, and yet he had the uplift-power of a first-class preacher. He spoke the way the average man could imagine himself speaking.

On the slavery issue Lincoln was firm, but he was no fire-eater. He was no abolitionist. In his debates against Douglas, when both were running for the Senate in 1858, he showed that he was about as conservative as an anti-slavery man could be. He tried to narrow down the whole slavery question simply to preventing slavery from spreading westward into the territories. The Founding Fathers, he explained, in their Northwest Ordinance of 1787 had prohibited slavery in what was then *their* West. Now, he said, to be true to their ideals, Americans must also keep slavery out of the newer West.

Himself of Southern ancestry, he did not hate the South. He believed in making every possible concession—short of allowing the spread of slavery. If anyone could have held the Union together, it would have been Lincoln. If an Abraham Lincoln—with Lincoln's shrewdness, with Lincoln's charity, with his generous understanding of the South and its problems, with his feeling for compromise—could not do it, the Union was surely beyond the help of politics.

The fateful presidential election of November 1860 confirmed widespread suspicions that there were no longer *national* parties. It convinced the South that their hope was not in words but in weapons. From ten Southern States, Lincoln received not a single electoral vote. In the Electoral College, Lincoln

A Southern view of Lincoln aided by the Devil. Even Lincoln's desk has cloven hoofs, and Lincoln himself is casually using the Constitution for a footstool.

carried all eighteen Free States, Breckenridge carried eleven Slave States, Douglas carried only Missouri (and also received a minority of New Jersey's split votes), and John Bell, a compromise candidate from Tennessee, carried three border Slave States. Although Lincoln easily won in the Electoral College (with 180 votes against 123 for all the others), he was not the choice of the majority of the American people. Lincoln received less than 40 percent of the popular vote. The other candidates all together had received nearly a million votes more than Lincoln. Lincoln had won, but the Union was in new peril.

When word of Lincoln's election reached South Carolina, the State seceded from the Union. She was quickly joined from the lower South by six other States: Mississippi, Florida, Alabama, Georgia, Louisiana, and Texas. Each declared its own independence. Then their delegates met in Montgomery, Alabama, in February 1861, even before Lincoln was inaugurated. They wrote a new constitution and announced that a new nation, the Confederate States of America, was born.

For them, the United States was now

a foreign nation. The seceded States therefore could no longer allow the United States to keep its arsenals and forts inside their borders. Using their own State troops, they at once began seizing federal posts. To avoid bloodshed, the United States troops withdrew to one of their strongest positions, a place in Charleston Harbor called Fort Sumter.

As soon as Lincoln was inaugurated on March 4, 1861, he had to make one of the great decisions in American history. Should he let the South take Fort Sumter and go its own way? That would mean no civil war. But it would also mean the end of the Union. Or should he reinforce the federal forts in the South, prepare for war, and lead a fight that might go on for years to keep all the States inside one great nation?

Lincoln decided to stand firm for the Union. He would fight if necessary, but he would let the South fire the first shot. He notified South Carolina that he was sending supplies to Fort Sumter. South Carolina then decided to take the fort before it was reinforced. At 4:20 A.M. on April 12, 1861, Confederate General P. G. T. Beauregard, a West Point graduate who had once fought for the Union in the Mexican War, began bombarding Fort Sumter from the Charleston shore batteries. At 2:30 P.M. the next afternoon Major Robert Anderson, also a West Point graduate who had fought alongside Beauregard in Mexico, surrendered the fort. No one had been wounded, but war had begun. The first, the quickest, and the most bloodless battle of the war was over. But it was no fair sample of what was to come.

CHAPTER 27

Everybody's War

This American Civil War was not quite like any war that had ever happened before. Half a nation fought against the other half over the freedom of a small minority. This itself was something new. It was as new, as strenuous, and as unpredictable as everything else in America. Leaving over 600,000 dead, the Civil War would be the bloodiest in all American history—and the bloodiest war in the whole world during the nineteenth century. Of every ten men who fought, four became casualties. No other modern nation paid so high a price to hold itself together.

Southerners did not see themselves simply as slave owners fighting to preserve their property, or as rebels trying to tear the Union apart. Instead they imagined they were fighting the American Revolution all over again. White Southerners, they said, were oppressed by Yankee tyrants. Men of the South were now playing the role of the gallant American colonists. Northerners were the oppressive British, and Abraham Lincoln was another George III. If the British government had no right to force American colonists to stay inside their empire, why did the United States government have any right to force Southern States to stay inside the Union?

Southerners said they were fighting for self-government. One flaw in this argument was that it left out the whole question of slavery. Self-government—*for* whom, and *by* whom? In 1860 there were nearly four million slaves in the Southern States. White Southerners who said they were fighting for their own right to govern themselves were also fighting *against* the right of Negroes to govern themselves. Of course, Fitzhugh and Calhoun and other defenders of slavery had not seen it quite that way. The Negro, they said, had no right to govern himself. Self-government was for white people only.

When Southerners said that all they wanted was to secede from the Union, they also gave themselves a military advantage. To win their point all they had to do was to declare their independence and to go their own way. On the other hand, the North would have to *force* the Southern States to obey the Union. The North would have to invade the South, occupy it, and subjugate it. The North had to attack.

At the beginning, many Northerners hopefully called it "the six months' war." They expected it to be over in short order. For the North seemed stronger in every way. Also they had been taught that the attacking army always had a great advantage. The textbooks the generals had studied when they were cadets at West Point explained that the way to win a war was to concentrate your forces on one or two points, and attack. Meanwhile the defenders would be weaker, because they would have to spread out their forces to protect against lots of possible assaults.

The old-fashioned weapons gave almost no advantage to the defenders. For the old smoothbore flintlock musket (which was standard equipment in the British army during the Revolution and in European armies even afterward) was inaccurate, it had a short range, and it was slow to reload. That meant that the attacking forces could come very close before the defenders could shoot them down, and most of them would get through before they could be hit. If, as Northern generals at first imagined, the North could only keep the advantage of the attack, they could win a few decisive battles, capture the enemy capital, and then the war would be over.

These generals were wrong. The war lasted four blood-soaked years. This new warfare would be as different from earlier American wars as an elephant is different from a mosquito.

A number of great changes made the difference. During the American Revolution, as we have seen, while the standard British weapon was the flintlock musket, many American backwoodsmen had begun using the rifle. But it was not until the Civil War that the rifle became the standard American army weapon. The textbooks which the Civil War generals had read at West Point came from the earlier age of the smoothbore flintlock.

The rifle was so called because the inside of its barrel was "rifled"—cut with spiral grooves. Then when the bullet was pushed out it was set spinning. This gave it a longer range (500 yards instead of 50 yards) and a much more accurate aim. Another improvement was the "caplock," which used a new chemical (fulminate of mercury) enclosed in a cap to make the explosion that sent the bullet. The caplock was reliable even when the old flintlock—which struck a piece of flint against steel to make a spark—would not have worked because of wet weather. Also the old muskets had been "muzzle-loaders," but the new rifle was a "breech-loader." This meant it loaded from the back near the trigger, which was much more convenient and quicker. There were even some rifles which were automatic. A single clip of bullets would fire many shots.

These new weapons gave a great new advantage to the defenders. In the old-fashioned war, a soldier was expected to carry on him all the ammunition he could use in a battle. The old muskets were so slow to load that it took some time before he could use up his ammunition. But with the fast-loading new rifles, the soldier could not keep shooting very long unless new supplies were being constantly brought up to him. This made some troublesome new problems—especially for the generals on the attack. To move ammunition became as important as to move men.

Now the defenders, with their accurate long-range rifles, sat protected behind battlements in well-supplied forts. Now they could pick off the attackers before these even came close. They could fire quickly again and again. But the attacking force was on the move. If they stopped to reload they were sitting ducks.

No more would armies confront each other in solid ranks. Everybody had to

A Northern recruiting poster dated only eight days after the firing on Fort Sumter.

take cover. Attackers had to spread out into small parties of skirmishers to make more dispersed targets. Now the "Indian" tactics, which Americans had tried against the British in the Revolution, would become common. But attacking soldiers now made instant fortifications—of logs, bales of hay, rocks, anything in sight—so they could pile their ammunition beside them and get some of the advantages of defenders.

Most important, they learned to make the earth itself into a fort by using the spade. This was the beginning of modern trench warfare. In the old days, generals thought it was cowardly for a

Federal troops destroying a Southern railway bridge.

soldier to hide in a hole in the ground. Now the soldier had no choice. When General Robert E. Lee ordered his men in the Army of Northern Virginia to work hard at digging trenches, at first they laughed at him as their "King of Spades." But they soon thanked him for giving them protection against enemy rifles. The axe and the spade were now as important as the gun. One man in a hole with an artillery battery behind him was worth three in the open.

The attacking army, then, had to carry enormous supplies of ammunition and had to build its own fortifications as it advanced. The railroad, which had never been used much in wars before, was now a great help. But once the supplies left the rails, they still had to be carried by horse or mule over bumpy roads and through mud.

In this kind of warfare, railroads were life lines. They were slow and hard to build, but quick and easy to cut. If you could cut the enemy's rails, he would eventually have to stop shooting. The Civil War therefore became more and more a war aimed at the enemy's communication lines. The first Battle of Bull Run (July 1861) was still very much like the old-fashioned warfare, with solid lines of soldiers standing up against each other to fight a "decisive" battle. By the time of the Battle of Petersburg three years later, the Union army was aiming at the Confederate railroads.

The new kind of warfare was a war of exhaustion. It was not enough to cut off the enemy's supplies by railroad. You also had to prevent his bringing in supplies by water. The South, as we have seen, was blessed with many rivers. At first it seemed that the Mississippi would be a God-given supply line behind the whole South.

But early in the war this hope was blasted when a bold move by the astonishing David Glasgow Farragut captured New Orleans for the Union. Farragut, the son of a naval officer, had been commissioned a midshipman at the age of nine, and had seen action in the War of 1812 when he was only eleven. His orders commanded him first to capture the two forts at the mouth of the Mississippi which protected New Orleans. But he disregarded orders and at one blow seized New Orleans itself by racing past the two forts (losing only three of his seventeen ships). Farragut took the city on April 26, 1862, almost before anyone knew he was in the neighborhood. Now the South could not bring in supplies from the Gulf of Mexico for its troops in the West.

The ocean and the Gulf of Mexico surrounded the Southern States. With several other good ports besides New Orleans, the South still had highways to the world. The North therefore had to block up the other Southern ports if the South was to be strangled. The South did wonders with its few ships by shielding them with iron and equipping them with steam-driven propellers. These had an advantage against old wooden sailing vessels similar to that which the new firearms had against the old. The new ironclad ships gave a great new advantage to the defense. Still the scores of Northern ships offshore harassed merchant vessels and kept them from reaching Southern ports.

The war of exhaustion hit everybody in the South, civilians as well as the military. The same ships that would have brought arms and ammunition to the armies also would have brought machinery for the factories and food and clothing and medical supplies for all. The Northern blockade against the South worked slowly but it worked surely. People called it the "Conda" after the Anaconda, the huge boa constrictor snake that kills its prey by squeezing.

The war of exhaustion was slow. It was not won by a few knockout blows like the Battle of Waterloo, but by deprivation and strangulation and starvation. As the struggle dragged on into its fourth year, European experts, who had never seen this kind of war before, began to think it was not war at all. One Prussian general sneered that he would not even study the battles of the war because they were nothing but "the combats of two armed mobs." Another Old World critic compared the North and South to two lunatics playing chess—both knew a few moves, yet neither understood the game.

But this kind of war was no longer a game. The old rules of war which the generals had learned at West Point were no longer of much use. It was everybody's war, with no holds barred. The winning generals turned out to be those, like U. S. Grant, who had never believed the old rules, or those, like William T. Sherman, who were good at forgetting them.

The long war was enough to try anybody's patience. Northern generals devised shortcuts. Of course, you could exhaust your enemy by cutting off his supplies, by wearing him down in one place after another. And that was Lincoln's large strategy. Surround the South, cut off the South from the world and the world's supplies, and then the South could not live. You could exhaust your enemy, too, simply by destroying him—by burning his crops and houses and destroying his factories, by tearing up his railroads and blowing up his bridges. Impatient Northern generals tried precisely this.

On May 7, 1864, Union General William T. Sherman set out southeastward from Chattanooga, Tennessee, on a march of destruction. Going through Georgia his army traveled light. He told his men to carry only their arms, for he figured that they would loot food and supplies along the way. This too would help exhaust the enemy, while it solved the problem of supply. He ordered them to move fast, without waiting to protect their rear. Sherman's army left a path of devastation three hundred miles wide all across Georgia. What was not worth carrying away they burned, what they could not burn they smashed.

Later General Sherman explained that what many people called "humanity" had no place in modern war. In the long run, so his argument went, the only way

The Civil War provided a vast variety of subject matter for a new generation of realistic artists. This engraving of a Northern sharpshooter was made from a sketch by Winslow Homer, the young artist-correspondent for Harper's Weekly.

to be humane—to get the war over—was to be cruel. The Confederate General Lee had warned his men that they should never hurt civilians. But modern war could not be won that way. The only up-to-date strategy, according to the brilliant Northerner Philip H. Sheridan whose victories had made him a general when he was barely thirty, was to punish every enemy—man, woman, and child. Leave them "nothing but their eyes to weep with." That was the new path to victory in the new kind of warfare.

It took four full years to exhaust the South. If the North had not been so much the stronger, it might have taken much longer. With twenty-three States against the South's eleven, with 22,000,000 people against the South's 9,000,000, the North had a big advantage. The North had more and better railroads, more ships, and more factories.

Also, while the North had lots of labor-saving devices like the reaper to free men for the army, the South depended for its labor on Negro slaves. These might any moment turn out to be a "fifth column"—an enemy force behind Southern lines—because they had very good reasons of their own for helping the enemy. Every third Southerner was

The war also provided rich, horrendous materials for pioneers in the new art of photography. This photograph shows a soldier killed at the Battle of Gettysburg.

a Negro. Southerners therefore lived in fear of a civil war all their own— if the Negroes ever decided to take up arms. Meanwhile, after the North finally decided in December 1862 to accept Negroes in its armed forces, it was strengthened by more than 180,000 Negroes fighting on its side. The North grew lots of different crops, while the South was glutted with a few staples— tobacco, cotton, and rice—which it had to export in order to obtain anything else.

Worst of all, the South suffered from delusions which prevented her seeing facts. Southerners were still astonished that any power on earth dared make war on the world's greatest producer of cotton. They had long told themselves: "Cotton is King." They imagined too that only Southerners were civilized, and that one Southerner "could whip a half-dozen Yankees and not half try." The South's grandiose dreams turned into nightmares.

In the North, too, it was everybody's war. There, too, nearly every family lost a soldier. And in quite new ways the gore was brought into everybody's home. For the first time in history, the battles were thoroughly covered by newspaper correspondents who telegraphed back eyewitness accounts so that civilians could read the horrors next morning at breakfast.

The New York *Herald* alone once had forty correspondents in the field, and spent a half-million dollars on them. Northern correspondents, who would have been shot as spies if discovered, smuggled themselves behind Southern lines disguised as women or as Confed-erate soldiers. When Albert D. Richardson of the New York *Tribune* traveled through the South in 1861, he sent back his dispatches through a New York bank in code. General William T. Sherman was so irritated at the crowd of correspondents around his headquarters that he threatened to shoot them. General Grant was more amiable and used the correspondents to give people the news he wanted them to believe. When some generals objected that the newspapers were giving away valuable information to the enemy, the New York *World* protested that this was a "people's war."

The pioneer photographer Mathew Brady and his large crew, at the risk of their lives, sent photographs back home to show everyone the battle action. Soldiers sometimes ran away from Brady's camera because they had never seen a camera before, and imagined it to be a new kind of gun. Brady's photographic buggy, which soldiers called the "What-Is-It?," was a conspicuous target. On several occasions, Brady barely escaped being killed. After the first Battle of Bull Run, Brady was lost for three days before finding his way back to Washington. There he quickly secured new equipment and rushed back to the battlefield.

In the "people's war" women played a new, important part. Dorothea Dix, the courageous New Englander who had braved public opinion to prevent cruelties to the insane, now followed the example of the Englishwoman Florence Nightingale. Miss Dix became the first Superintendent of Army Nurses. She was a strict manager and enlisted only women who were strong and not too good-looking. In those days, it took

THE INFLUENCE OF WOMAN

Soldiers Shirts

THE SISTER OF CHARITY

HOME TIDINGS

"*Our Women and the War,*" *another view of the varied American scene by Winslow Homer.*

gumption to find any place for women in the army, and she was the pioneer. Women were so anxious to do their part that some four hundred of them pretended to be soldiers until they were discovered.

Although it was everybody's war, the leaders did much to turn the tide. If Jefferson Davis had been President of the United States and Lincoln had been President of the Confederacy, would the North still have won?

Lincoln was a stronger leader. As a politician, he knew how important it was, in everybody's war, to keep everybody's support. At the beginning of the war, in order to keep the support of the border Slave States—Delaware, Maryland, Kentucky, and Missouri—Lincoln had refused to emancipate the slaves. But in late 1862, when the war was going badly for the North, he felt the time had come to show the great moral purpose of the war, and to try to secure foreign support. On January 1, 1863, he issued the Emancipation Proclamation. It freed the slaves, but only in the States that were rebelling against the United States. The freeing of all the slaves would have to wait until after the war.

Just as the Declaration of Independence had helped unite the colonists and

Lee, Grant, and their staffs at Appomattox.

helped persuade the world, so the Emancipation Proclamation did its work. "Mr. Lincoln's cause," wrote an English merchant on hearing of the Proclamation, "is just and holy, the cause of truth, and of universal humanity." English workingmen held mass meetings to support the Union. Now there was little danger that the British government would recognize or support the Confederacy. This was not merely a war for Union, but a war against slavery.

Lincoln was not afraid of new ideas. He tried one general after another until he found U. S. Grant. Of course, it was partly good luck that Grant happened to be there. But Lincoln was willing to try his luck on a general who usually looked a mess and who did not insist on

waging war according to the textbooks he had studied at West Point. Lincoln believed that a new world needed new ideas. General Grant agreed. He had a notion of how new the new warfare had become. And he had the advantage that he was a hard man to predict.

After General Sherman's march of devastation through Georgia and the Carolinas, the South was still not quite defeated. But she was exhausted. She had no strength to go on. Then at last when the railroad to the Confederate capital of Richmond was cut, Richmond had to be abandoned. In a final battle at Appomattox, General Grant overwhelmed Lee's force.

On the afternoon of April 9, 1865, the Confederate General Lee, accompanied only by his military secretary, rode his horse to a little white house in the town of Appomattox Court House on the Appomattox River in central Virginia. He went to arrange his surrender. There occurred one of the most remarkable, and one of the most encouraging, episodes in American history. It would show that, despite the monstrous indecencies of war, the respect of one American for another had not been destroyed.

Grant, who had just come in from the field, was dusty and even more unkempt than usual. Confronting him in the living room of the house he had taken for his headquarters was General Lee—handsome, erect, in a spotless uniform, and wearing his dress sword. The men sat down and then exchanged recollections of their fighting together twenty years before in the Mexican War. The two great generals talked to each other with calmness, courtesy, and respect.

Now that the fighting was over, it seemed that humanity had suddenly returned. Lee heard Grant's terms of surrender. Grant was more generous than he needed to be. He allowed Southern officers to keep their swords—the symbols of their honor—and he allowed officers and men to keep their horses, so they could go home and plant their crops. Lee was touched. "This," he said, "will have a very happy effect upon my army."

A renewed nation, fused in the fires of war, would now seek its destiny in peace.

FOR FURTHER READING

More about the people and the years covered in this book may be found in other Landmark Giants, as well as Landmark and World Landmark Books. The Landmark titles below correspond with the five parts of this book.

Part One: An Assortment of Plantations

The Continent We Live On by Ivan T. Sanderson, adapted by Anne Terry White

Prehistoric America by Anne Terry White

The American Indian by William Brandon, adapted by Anne Terry White, foreword by John F. Kennedy

The Vikings by Elizabeth Janeway

The Voyages of Christopher Columbus by Armstrong Sperry

Captain Cortés Conquers Mexico by William Johnson

Walter Raleigh: Man of Two Worlds by Henrietta Buckmaster

The Voyages of Henry Hudson by Eugene Rachlis

The Story of the Thirteen Colonies by Clifford Lindsey Alderman

Life in Colonial America by Elizabeth George Speare

Pocahontas and Captain John Smith by Marie Lawson

The Landing of the Pilgrims by James Daugherty

The Witchcraft of Salem Village by Shirley Jackson

Peter Stuyvesant of Old New York by Anna and Russel Crouse

The Explorations of Père Marquette by Jim Kjelgaard

William Penn: Quaker Hero by Hildegarde Dolson

Evangeline and the Acadians by Robert Tallant

The Hudson's Bay Company by Richard Morenus

Famous Pirates of the New World by A. B. C. Whipple

Part Two: Thirteen States Are Born

The Story of New England by Monroe Stearns

Rogers' Rangers and the French and Indian War by Bradford Smith

The American Revolution by Bruce Bliven, Jr.

George Washington: Frontier Colonel by Sterling North

Thomas Jefferson: Father of Democracy by Vincent Sheean

Ben Franklin of Old Philadelphia by Margaret Cousins

Paul Revere and the Minute Men by Dorothy Canfield Fisher

Ethan Allen and the Green Mountain Boys by Slater Brown

The Winter at Valley Forge by F. Van Wyck Mason

John Paul Jones, Fighting Sailor by Armstrong Sperry

The Marquis de Lafayette: Bright Sword for Freedom by Hodding Carter

The Swamp Fox of the Revolution by Stewart H. Holbrook

Betsy Ross and the Flag by Jane Mayer

Our Independence and the Constitution by Dorothy Canfield Fisher

Part Three: American Ways of Growing; & Part Four: Thinking Like Americans

Part Five: The Rocky Road to Union

INDEX

Daniel J. Boorstin is Distinguished Service Professor of American History at the University of Chicago. His most extensive work, *The Americans,* is a sweeping new view of American history, revealing in the story of our past some of the special character of the American experience. The first volume, *The Americans: The Colonial Experience,* won Columbia University's Bancroft Prize. The second volume, *The Americans: The National Experience,* in 1966 received the Parkman Prize of the Society of American Historians as the book that best combined historical scholarship with literary excellence. Mr. Boorstin is now at work on the third and final volume, to be entitled *The Americans: The World Experience.*

He is also the editor of *An American Primer* (in two volumes) and of the 25-volume *Chicago History of American Civilization* series.